12.37

DATE DUE

992		

Themes in the
Social Sciences

*Culture and communication:
the logic by which symbols
are connected*

Themes in the Social Sciences

Editors: *Jack Goody & Geoffrey Hawthorn*

The aim of this series is to publish books which will focus on topics of general and interdisciplinary interest in the social sciences. They will be concerned with non-European cultures and with developing countries, as well as with industrial societies. The emphasis will be on comparative sociology and, initially, on sociological, anthropological and demographic topics. These books are intended for undergraduate teaching, but not as basic introductions to the subjects they cover. Authors have been asked to write on central aspects of current interest which have a wide appeal to teachers and research students, as well as to undergraduates.

First books in the series

Edmund Leach: *Culture and Communication: the logic by which symbols are connected*
   An introduction to the use of structuralist analysis in social anthropology

Anthony Heath: *Rational Choice and Social Exchange*
   A critique of exchange theory

Culture & communication

the logic by which symbols are connected

An introduction to the use of
structuralist analysis in
social anthropology
by Edmund Leach

Professor of Social Anthropology,
University of Cambridge

Cambridge University Press

Cambridge
London   New York   Melbourne

Published by the Syndics of the Cambridge University Press
The Pitt Building, Trumpington Street, Cambridge CB2 1RP
Bentley House, 200 Euston Road, London NW1 2DB
32 East 57th Street, New York, NY 10022, USA
296 Beaconsfield Parade, Middle Park, Melbourne 3206, Australia

© Cambridge University Press 1976

Library of Congress catalogue card number: 75-30439

ISBN 0 521 21131 X hard covers
ISBN 0 521 29052 X paperback

First published 1976
Reprinted 1976 (twice)

Typeset by Vail-Ballou Press, Inc., Binghamton, New York
Printed in the United States of America by R. R. Donnelley
& Sons Company, Crawfordsville, Indiana

Contents

Culture and communication:
the logic by which symbols
are connected

Introduction

The presumed average reader of this essay is an undergraduate who is just beginning to make contact with the literature of social anthropology. Some such potential readers, and perhaps some of their teachers as well, are very likely to be put off by the formalism and superficial difficulty of the argument in the opening sections, so I must justify my presentation.

Many years ago I incurred the odium of senior anthropological colleagues by daring to suggest that other people's ethnography is often very dull. I was misunderstood but I persist in my heresy.

The work of the social anthropologist consists in the analysis and interpretation of ethnographic fact, customary behaviour as directly observed. The most fundamental way in which the procedures of modern anthropologists differ from those of their predecessors a hundred years ago is that the modern treatment of ethnographic evidence is always functionalist. Today, every detail of custom is seen as part of a complex; it is recognised that details, considered in isolation, are as meaningless as isolated letters of the alphabet. So ethnography has ceased to be an inventory of custom, it has become the art of thick description; the intricate interweaving of plot and counterplot as in the work of a major novelist (Geertz (1973)).

And if we grant that, it is plain that no detail of an anthropologist's own fieldwork could ever seem dull; detail is the very essence. But the details of other people's fieldwork are perhaps another matter.

Only in very rare instances are anthropological monographs written in such a way that the reader can pick up a comprehensive feeling for the alien cultural environment in which the events described take place. Yet in the absence of such an atmosphere an overload of detail simply intensifies incomprehensibility.

How then should untravelled undergraduates be introduced to the mysteries of social anthropology?

The usual procedure is by means of potted ethnographies – simplified summaries such as are provided by the admirable and widely-read series 'Case Studies in Cultural Anthropology' (Holt, Rinehart and Winston, Inc.) and by textbooks which illustrate general propositions

1

by means of isolated examples lifted, out of context, from classic anthropological monographs relating to the Nuer, the Tikopia, the Tallensi, the Trobriands or what have you. Both devices are a cheat. The novice reader is misled into thinking that the facts are far less complicated than is really the case and may easily come to the conclusion that there is nothing in the subject matter of social anthropology that could not easily be understood by a child of ten.

The alternative approach which I have adopted in the present case is to assume that the only ethnography about which a novice social anthropologist is likely to have any intimate knowledge is that which derives from his or her own life experience. Of set purpose my essay contains very few examples of ethnographic fact and those that it does contain are commonplace; almost the only ethnographic monograph to which the reader is asked to pay close attention is the Bible. Instead, it is hoped that each individual reader will draw on personal experience to illustrate the argument.

By now my general thesis is becoming very familiar: culture communicates; the complex interconnectedness of cultural events itself conveys information to those who participate in those events. That granted, my purpose is to suggest a systematic procedure by which the participant observer anthropologist can set about decoding the messages embedded in the complexities which he observes. The methodology can only be seen to be useful if it is applied to complex materials. Each reader must seek out an appropriate complex of ethnographic fact for himself.

All the ideas in this essay are borrowed from others; the only thing that is original about the argument is the form in which it is cast. But the essay is about the semantics of cultural forms and since the form is my own so also is the meaning.

2

1. *Empiricists and rationalists: economic transactions and acts of communication*

In this section I shall delimit my field.

As you can see from its title, the essay which I have listed in the bibliography under Mary Douglas (1972) bears directly on my theme. In comment on a famous paper concerning the seasonal life of the Eskimo published at the beginning of the century (Mauss and Beuchat (1906)) Douglas writes as follows:

> '[It] is an explicit attack on geographical or technological determinism in interpreting domestic organization. It demands an ecological approach in which the structure of ideas and of society, the mode of gaining a livelihood and the domestic architecture are interpreted as a single interacting whole in which no one element can be said to determine the other.'

Thus described, the Eskimo paper may be considered a prototype for what every British social anthropologist would like to do with the ethnographic data which fill his notebooks. In practice the monographs which anthropologists write seldom preserve this kind of balance. According to the predilections of the author we find that special stress is laid *either* on the structure of ideas, *or* on the structure of society, *or* on the mode of gaining a livelihood, and the principle that we are all the time dealing with 'a single interacting whole' is easily forgotten.

It is also easy to forget that contrasted predilections of individual authors are themselves part of a single interacting whole.

All social anthropologists take as their subject matter the *variety* of human culture and society, and they all assume that their task is not only to describe what the varieties are but to explain why they exist. There are many different kinds of 'explanation' and a preference for one kind rather than another is largely a matter of personal prejudice.

Some anthropologists evidently feel that all explanation must be in terms of cause and effect. Scholars of this sort concentrate their attention on the historical account of antecedent events. Others hold that the essence of the matter is to understand the interdependence of different parts of the system as it exists at the present time; these offer structural–functionalist explanations. For others again the object of the exercise is to show how any particular cultural institution, as

3

actually observed, is only one of a set of possible permutations and combinations, some of which can also be directly observed in other cultural settings. These last offer structuralist explanations – using the term 'structuralist' in the sense favoured by Lévi-Strauss.

But before you can hope to explain anything you need to understand what is going on. What are the facts which need to be explained? On this issue most contemporary discussion among social anthropologists exhibits a tension between two contrasted attitudes, empiricist and rationalist.

The empiricist position is perhaps best represented by the 'transactional' viewpoint of Fredrik Barth (1966) which is a development from the functionalist tradition originally established by Malinowski and Raymond Firth, which in turn is quite close to the structural–functionalism of Radcliffe-Brown, Fortes and Gluckman and their many intellectual descendants. Empiricists assume that the basic task of the anthropologist in the field is to record directly-observed, face-to-face behaviours of members of a local community interacting with one another in their day-to-day activities.

This localised field of human activity is then analysed as one in which *social persons*, acting out the customary conventions associated with their particular roles and statuses, engage in economic transactions. The economic transactions carry implication for our understanding of the system of manifest political, legal and religious institutions within which the community operates. In this case, what is described as the 'social structure' of the system is a derivation from sets of such directly observed transactions. Empiricist anthropologists steer clear of argument about 'the structure of ideas current within a society' which most of them would consider to be a second order, unobservable, abstraction invented by theoreticians.

In monographs written by anthropologists who work in this empiricist (functionalist) tradition, 'social structures' are commonly exhibited as patterns of kinship and descent. This is simply because it is manifestly the case that, in nearly all self-perpetuating face-to-face communities, kinship relationships provide the primary network through which economic transactions can be seen to flow. In consequence kinship relations are viewed as a 'transformation' of economic relations.

The contrasted rationalist standpoint is prototypically represented by the work of Lévi-Strauss and by some of the later writings of Evans-Pritchard.

The rationalism in question is not that of Descartes, who believed that by following rigorous procedures of logical argument we can develop in the mind a 'true' model of the universe which exactly corresponds to the phenomenal objective universe which we perceive through our senses, but something closer to the 'new science' of Giambattista Vico, the eighteenth-century Italian philosopher, which

4

recognised that the imaginative operations of human minds are 'poetic' and are not trammelled by fixed, easily specified rules of Aristotelian and mathematical logic.

Lévi-Straussian rationalists call themselves 'structuralists', but structure here refers to the structure of ideas rather than the structure of society.

Because of their interest in ideas as opposed to objective facts rationalist anthropologists tend to be more concerned with what is said than with what is done. In field research they attach particular importance to mythology and to informants' statements about what ought to be the case. Where there is discrepancy between verbal statements and observed behaviour, rationalists tend to maintain that the social reality 'exists' in the verbal statements rather than in what actually happens.

The justification for this position may be illustrated by an analogy. A Beethoven symphony 'exists' as a musical score which can be interpreted in all sorts of ways by all sorts of orchestras. The fact that a particularly incompetent performance diverges widely from the score as written does not lead us to say that the 'real' symphony was the bad performance rather than the ideal score.

In the thinking of rationalist (structuralist) social anthropologists the 'structure' of a system of social ideas bears the same sort of relationship to what actually happens as does a musical score to the performance. The score is, in a sense, the 'cause' of what happens, but we cannot work backwards and reliably infer the score from direct observation of any single performer's behaviour. In the musical case, the score originates 'in the mind' of the composer. By analogy, committed rationalists tend to write of cultural systems being composed by a kind of collectivity – 'the human mind'. From this they infer that it is necessary to study a number of contrasted empirical examples (a number of separate performances by separate orchestras) before we can be confident that we know what is the common abstract 'reality' which underlies them all.

For those who adopt this approach, the directly observed interactions between individuals, which the functionalist empiricist perceives as *economic transactions*, are reinterpreted as *acts of communication*.

But here let me remind you of what I said earlier on. The rival theories of anthropologists are themselves parts of a single interacting whole. Both viewpoints accept the central dogma of functionalism that cultural details must always be viewed in context, that everything is meshed in with everything else. In this regard the two approaches, the empiricist (functionalist) and the rationalist (structuralist), are complementary rather than contradictory; one is a transformation of the other.

According to Malinowski, the Founding Father of functionalist–

5

empiricist anthropology, 'the principle of reciprocity' pervades all social behaviour. In saying this he was concerned to emphasise that the economic transactions which flow from reciprocity are socially cohesive, but he also recognised that reciprocity is a mode of communication. It not only does something, it says something.

If I give you a present you will feel morally bound to give something back. In economic terms you are in debt to me, but in communicative terms the sense of reciprocal obligation is an expression of a mutual feeling that we both belong to the same social system. Moreover, the way you reciprocate my gift will say something about our mutual relations. If you return my gift in kind by an exact equivalent, a glass of beer for a glass of beer, a greetings card for a greetings card, the behaviour expresses equality of status. But if the reciprocity involves gifts which are different in kind – I give you labour effort, you give me wages – the behaviour expresses inequality of status, employee versus employer.

And just to reinforce this point that the two anthropological viewpoints which I have here summarised as 'empiricist' and 'rationalist' are to be regarded as complementary rather than right or wrong I would emphasise that my own work includes specimen monographs of both types. Leach (1954) is rationalist in style; Leach (1961) is empiricist.

For the remainder of this essay the bias of argument will be structuralist (rationalist) rather than functionalist (empiricist). My general theme is communication; but that is simply for purposes of exposition. In practical affairs communication and economics can never be separated. Even in such a palpably symbolic communicative performance as that in which the priest in a Christian Mass offers the communicants bread and wine and declares that the bread and the wine are (respectively) the body and the blood of Jesus Christ there is an economic substratum. Someone, at some point, has to purchase the bread and wine.

However, by concentrating on the communicative aspects of transactions I can restrict the variety of parameters that I need to take into account. Within this limited frame of reference individual items of observed behaviour and individual details of custom can be treated as analogous to the words and sentences of a language, or passages in a musical performance.

In the case of ordinary language or ordinary musical performance any particular 'utterance' has originated in a human mind and the central puzzle is to determine how far the 'meaning' which is conveyed to the listener is the same as that which was intended by the originator. My present concern is to discuss how anthropologists, as observers, should set about the business of deciding what customs, other than verbal customs, can be said to 'mean'.

6

If we are to discuss this matter in other than the most general terms it is necessary to develop an artificial formal frame of reference; we must approach the issue almost as if it were a problem in mathematics. So the next three Sections of this book will be devoted to developing a jargon apparatus, a framework of concepts, which can serve as tools of analysis. If you are not used to argument which is presented in this formal schematic way you are likely to be put off. All that I can say in defence of such procedure is that it works. If you can accustom yourself to handling ethnographic evidence in the way I suggest you will find that many things will become comprehensible which had previously appeared to be just a chaos of random images.

2. Problems of terminology

When we are in the company of close friends and neighbours we all take it for granted that communication is a complex continuous process which has many non-verbal as well as verbal components. It is only when we meet with strangers that we suddenly become aware that, because all customary behaviours (and not just acts of speech) convey information, we cannot understand what is going on until we know the code. How then should we set about decoding other people's customs?

We can usefully distinguish three aspects of human behaviour:

(1) *natural biological activities of the human body* – breathing, heartbeat, metabolic process and so on;

(2) *technical actions*, which serve to alter the physical state of the world out there – digging a hole in the ground, boiling an egg;

(3) *expressive actions*, which either simply say something about the state of the world as it is, or else purport to alter it by metaphysical means.

Besides ordinary verbal utterances, expressive actions obviously include gestures, such as nodding the head, pulling faces and waving the arms, but they also include such behaviours as wearing a uniform, standing on a dais, and putting on a wedding ring.

My three *aspects* of behaviour are never completely separable. Even the act of breathing is 'expressive' – it 'says' that I am still alive. Even the simplest technical action has both biological and expressive implication. If I make myself a cup of coffee it not only alters the state of the world out-there, it also stimulates my internal metabolic processes, and it 'says' something. The way I prepare the coffee and the instruments which I use in the process give information about my cultural background.

The modes and channels through which we communicate with one another are very diverse and very complex but as a first approximation, for purposes of initial analysis, I shall assert that:

Human communication is achieved by means of expressive actions which operate as *signals*, *signs* and *symbols*. Most of us do not distinguish these three commonplace words at all precisely, and even

9

those who do may use them in widely different ways,* but in this essay they will be given specially defined meaning which I shall presently spell out.

In some forms of communication the expressive action of the sender is directly interpreted by the receiver. I speak, you listen; I nod my head, you see me do so. But in other cases the link is indirect. I write a letter and produce a pattern of signs and symbols on a piece of paper; some time later you receive the paper and interpret what I wrote.

The scope of indirect communication of this latter sort is very wide. We spend our whole time interpreting the results of the past expressive actions of other people. I can recognise that a church is not just an ordinary dwelling house simply by looking at it, but the 'expressive actions' which built in the distinction in the first place took place a long time ago.

In what follows I shall assume that *all* the various non-verbal dimensions of culture, such as styles in clothing, village lay-out, architecture, furniture, food, cooking, music, physical gestures, postural attitudes and so on are organised in patterned sets so as to incorporate coded information in a manner analogous to the sounds and words and sentences of a natural language. I assume therefore it is just as meaningful to talk about the grammatical rules which govern the wearing of clothes as it is to talk about the grammatical rules which govern speech utterances.

Clearly this is a very sweeping kind of assumption and I shall not

---

* The technical literature on this topic is very large and reaches back for several centuries. The most frequently cited 'authorities' are C. S. Peirce, F. de Saussure, E. Cassirer, L. Hjelmslev, C. Morris, R. Jakobson, R. Barthes. These authors ring the changes with the terms *sign, symbol, index, signal, icon,* with very little agreement as to how the categories should be related but with ever increasing complexity of argument. Firth (1973) follows Peirce and Morris in making *sign* a box category within which *symbol, signal, index* and *icon* are subdivisions. I have preferred the schema set out in Fig. 1 (p. 12) which is based on Mulder and Hervey (1972). Here *symbol* and *sign* are contrasted sub-sets of *index*. I have rejected Firth's usage because I need to take account of the major insights of de Saussure, Jakobson and Barthes. I have modified Mulder and Hervey, partly because I need a terminology which can be adapted to non-verbal as well as verbal communication, and partly I am more concerned to achieve comprehensibility than total rigour of argument. References to the authors mentioned above will be found in the Bibliography. Another helpful guide in this terminological maze is Fernandez (1965, 917–22); (1974).

10

attempt to justify it in detail. The basic argument is that the messages which we receive in different modes (through our various senses of touch, sight, hearing, smell, taste etc.) are readily transformed into other modes. Thus we can visualise what we hear in words; we can convert written texts into speech; a musician can transform the visual patterns of a musical score into movements of the arms, mouth and fingers. Evidently, at some deeply abstract level, all our different senses are coded in the same way. There *must* be some kind of 'logical' mechanism which allows us to transform sight messages into sound messages or touch messages or smell messages, and vice versa.

However, it is also important to recognise that there are major differences between the way individuals convey information to one another by the use of ordinary speech and by the written word, and the way we communicate with one another by coded conventions of non-verbal behaviour and non-verbal signs and symbols.

The grammatical rules which govern speech utterances are such that anyone with a fluent command of a language can generate spontaneously entirely new sentences with the confident expectation that he will be understood by his audience. This is *not* the case with most forms of non-verbal communication. Customary conventions can only be understood if they are familiar. A private symbol generated in a dream or in a poem, or a newly invented 'symbolic statement' of a non-verbal kind, will fail to convey information to others until it has been explained by other means. This shows that the syntax of non-verbal 'language' must be a great deal simpler than that of spoken or written language. Indeed, were this not the case, a short essay such as this on such a complex theme would be a complete waste of time.

So in reading what follows you need to remember that there is only an analogic similarity between the generation of new sentences by an individual engaged in spontaneous discourse and the generation of new customs by a cultural community over a period of time. In point of fact we understand very little about either.

My starting point is arbitrary. Let us call any unit of communication a 'communication event'. Any such event is dyadic (two-faced) in at least two senses:

(i) There must always be two individuals: X, the 'sender', the originator of the expressive action, and Y, the 'receiver', the interpreter of the product of the expressive action. X and Y may be in the same place at the same time or they may not.

(ii) The expressive action itself always has two aspects, simply because it transmits a message. On the one hand there is the action itself or the product of the action, the nodding of the head or the written letter, on the other there is the message which is encoded by the sender and decoded by the receiver.

11

The complexities of terminology which I have set out in Fig. 1 are analytically useful because the relationship between the 'message bearing entity A' and the 'message B' may assume a variety of forms. In reading the next few paragraphs I suggest that you refer repeatedly to Fig. 1.

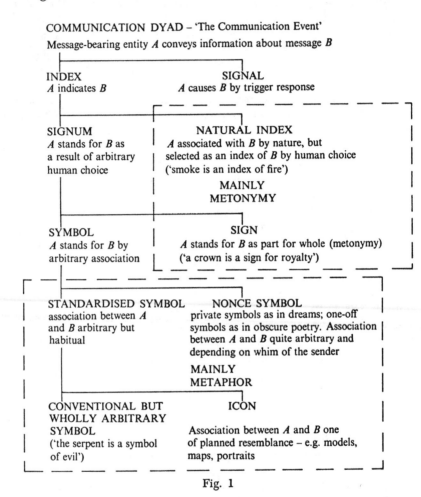

COMMUNICATION DYAD – 'The Communication Event'
Message-bearing entity *A* conveys information about message *B*

INDEX
A indicates *B*

SIGNAL
A causes *B* by trigger response

SIGNUM
A stands for *B* as
a result of arbitrary
human choice

NATURAL INDEX
A associated with *B* by nature, but
selected as an index of *B* by human choice
('smoke is an index of fire')

MAINLY
METONYMY

SYMBOL
A stands for *B* by
arbitrary association

SIGN
A stands for *B* as part for whole (metonymy)
('a crown is a sign for royalty')

STANDARDISED SYMBOL
association between *A*
and *B* arbitrary but
habitual

NONCE SYMBOL
private symbols as in dreams; one-off
symbols as in obscure poetry. Association
between *A* and *B* quite arbitrary and
depending on whim of the sender

MAINLY
METAPHOR

CONVENTIONAL BUT
WHOLLY ARBITRARY
SYMBOL
('the serpent is a symbol
of evil')

ICON

Association between *A* and *B* one
of planned resemblance – e.g. models,
maps, portraits

Fig. 1

The key distinctions in this schema are as follows:

SIGNAL   The relationship *A* : *B* is mechanical and automatic. *A* triggers *B*. The message and the message-bearing entity are simply two aspects of the same thing. All animals including human beings are constantly responding to a great variety of signals all the time.

INDEX   'A indicates B'. Signals are dynamic; indices static. Signals are causal; indices descriptive. Within this general class,

12

natural indices are those in which the association is natural – 'smoke is an index of fire', *signa* are those in which the association is a cultural convention; *symbols* and *signs* are then contrasted as sub-categories of *signa*.

So far I have more or less followed Mulder and Hervey (1972, 13–17). But the concern of these authors is to produce a rigorous analysis of the concept of *sign* in *linguistics*, and their lack of interest in non-verbal modes of communication limits the utility of the rest of their terminological system so far as my present purposes are concerned.

Mulder and Hervey distinguish *symbols* as '*signa* dependent on a separate (occasional) definition for their correct interpretation – e.g. *x, y, z* in an algebraic equation', and *signs* as '*signa* with wholly fixed conventional denotation, e.g. $+$, $-$, $=$ in an algebraic equation'. According to these definitions proper names are symbols while classifying nouns are signs. For example in the statement: 'That man is called John', *John* is a symbol for *that man*, but in 'those animals are pigs', *pigs* is a sign for *those animals*. Although this distinction between 'separately defined denotation' and 'wholly fixed conventional denotation' applies also to the *symbol/sign* contrast in my own Fig. 1, I am interested in a different aspect of this contrast and I shall spell out my definitions in a different way.

However, before I do that, it may be noted that Mulder and Hervey's algebraic example immediately makes it clear that any particular 'symbolic statement' is likely to be a combination of both symbols and signs, e.g. $x + y = z$.

It is also evident that whether a particular *signum* is to be regarded as a *sign* or a *symbol* will depend upon how it is used. The letters of the Roman alphabet when used in mathematical equations are *symbols* but when used in the context of verbal transcription they have approximately fixed conventional phonetic values and become *signs*. In this latter context, any particular letter standing by itself is meaningless, yet in combination sub-sets of the twenty-six available letter-signs can be made to represent hundreds of thousands of different words in hundreds of different languages.

For my purposes this is the heart of the matter. The two key points are (i) signs do not occur in isolation; a sign is always a member of a set of contrasted signs which function within a specific cultural context; (ii) a sign only conveys information when it is combined with other signs and symbols from the same context. Example: $x + y = z$ implies a mathematical context. Outside that context the signs $+$ and $=$ would convey no information. Putting the same point differently: *signs* are always *contiguous* to other signs which are members of the same set.

This gives us the definitions shown on Fig. 1.

13

(1) A *signum* is a *sign* when there is an intrinsic prior relationship between *A* and *B* because they belong to the same cultural context.
Examples:
(i)   Given the context of the sound transcription of spoken English by means of letters of the Roman alphabet, each letter or pair of letters is a *sign* for a particular sound.
(ii) Given the conventions of English spelling, the letter sequence APPLE is a *sign* for a particular fruit.
(iii) In the expression 'A stands for APPLE' *A* is a *sign* for APPLE and hence also a *sign* for the fruit.
(iv) Given the context of European political traditions in which the principal item of the ruling monarch's regalia was a crown, a crown is a *sign* for sovereignty.

This kind of relationship is sometimes described as *metonymy* and this is the sense in which I shall be using this word in this essay. Very roughly, as my last two examples suggest, *metonymy* is where 'a part stands for a whole'; the index which functions as a sign is contiguous to and part of that which is signified. Note that natural indices (e.g. 'smoke indicates fire') entail *metonymic* relationships as well as signs.

(2) Correspondingly: a *signum* is a *symbol* when *A* stands for *B* and there is *no* intrinsic prior relationship between *A* and *B*, that is to say *A* and *B* belong to different cultural contexts.
Examples:
(i)   In the algebraic proposition 'Let *x* stand for the price of cheese, *y* for the price of butter, and *z* for the price of bread. . .' *x*, *y* and *z* are symbols. Here, *x*, *y*, *z* belong to the context of mathematics, the prices belong to the context of the market place.
(ii) Where a crown is used as a trade mark for a brand of beer, it is a symbol not a sign. There is no prior intrinsic relationship. Crowns and beer come from different contexts.
(iii) In the Bible story the Serpent in the Garden of Eden is a symbol for Evil. The zoological context of serpents has no *intrinsic* relationship to the moral context of the concept of Evil.

In my Fig. 1, as is shown by the two dotted rectangles, the contrast between the *intrinsic* relationships entailed in natural indices and signs and the *non-intrinsic* relationships entailed in symbols corresponds to the distinction between *metonymy* and *metaphor*. Where *metonymy* implies contiguity, *metaphor* depends upon asserted similarity.
    Within the general category *symbol*, my schema again partly

14

follows Mulder and Hervey. *Standardised symbols* which convey information in the public domain are distinguished from *nonce symbols*, i.e. private one-off symbols, such as may appear in dreams or in poetry, which convey no public information until they are provided with an additional gloss. Within the broad category of *standardised symbols*, I distinguish *icons*, where the relation *A/B* is one of planned resemblance – e.g. models, maps, portraits – from *conventional but wholly arbitrary symbols*. This is a normal usage (see, e.g. Firth, 1973).

My point that *sign* relationships are contiguous and thus mainly *metonymic* while *symbol* relationships are arbitrary assertions of similarity and therefore mainly *metaphoric* needs further elaboration.

Almost everyone who has made a careful study of the processes of human communication is agreed that a distinction of this sort is analytically important, but again there are wide differences of terminology.

The usage *metaphor/metonymy* is due to Jakobson (1956). Lévi-Strauss (1966), in the tradition of de Saussure, describes almost the same distinction by the terms *paradigmatic/syntagmatic*. We meet much the same contrast in music when *harmony*, in which different instruments make simultaneous noises which are heard in combination, is distinguished from *melody* in which one note follows another to form a tune.

In music we are familiar with the idea of a melody being transposed into a different key so that it can be played by a different instrument, but this is simply a special case of a very general process by which syntagmatic chains of signs linked by metonymy can be shifted by paradigmatic transposition (metaphor) into a different manifest form. Prototype examples of *syntagmatic chains* are the letters forming a written word, or the words forming a sentence, or the sequence of musical notes written on a musical score to indicate a 'tune'.

An example of *paradigmatic association* is provided by the simultaneous transposition which occurs when a sequence of musical notes is interpreted as a sequence of finger movements across the keyboard of a piano, which, by further conversion, become a sequential pattern of sound waves reaching the ear of the listener. The relation between the written score, the finger movements and the sound waves is *paradigmatic*.

The jargon is tiresome but at times useful. Approximately, but not exactly, the following equivalents apply:
Symbol/Sign = Metaphor/Metonymy =
Paradigmatic association/Syntagmatic chain = Harmony/Melody.

It is our common experience that all kinds of human action, and not just speaking, serve to convey information. Such modes of communication include writing, musical performance, dancing, painting, singing, building, acting, curing, worshipping and so on. The whole argument of this essay rests on the proposition that, at some level, the 'mechanism' of these various modes of communication must be the same, that each is a 'transformation' of every other in much the same sense as a written text is a transformation of speech. If this really is the case then we need a language in which to discuss the attributes of this common code. That is where my jargon comes in.

3. Objects, sense-images, concepts

A fundamental difficulty in this whole business is that we are concerned all the time with the operations of human minds as well as with objects and actions in the world out-there.

The music which results from the pianist's transformation of notes in the score to finger movements on the keyboard is not a simple consequence of signalled trigger responses. Trigger responses are involved but they are modulated by the musical thought and competence of the performer. And the same applies to the whole range of human communication, both verbal and non-verbal. Whenever we discuss the 'meaning' of expressive behaviour we are concerned with the relationship between observable patterns in the world out-there and unobservable patterns 'in the mind'. But here we come back again to the opposition between rationalism and empiricism. What do we really mean by 'patterns in the mind'? I would urge you to be sceptical.

Only a very extreme behaviourist psychologist would want to discuss problems of meaning without allowing *some* degree of 'reality' to the operations of mental ideas but the opposite form of distortion is all too common. Much of the theory of signs and symbols (semiology) has been developed by European followers of de Saussure, and they have grappled with the problem of the relationship between ideas and external objects by adopting the extreme rationalist position that we can ignore the external objects altogether.

These writers insist that we need to distinguish carefully between 'words considered as external objects' – i.e. patterns of sound waves, patterns of marks on paper – and 'words as sound images'. You yourself have a personal experience of 'words as sound images' every time you 'think' in words without uttering sounds or moving the lips. So far as your mother tongue is concerned every word (as sound image) is indissolubly linked with an internalised mental representation or concept. Following this line of argument the term *linguistic sign*, in the writings of de Saussure and his followers, refers to a combination of sound image and concept. The linguistic sign is a single entity with two facets, like the two sides of a sheet of paper, (i) the sound

17

image (Fr. *significant*, 'the signifying') and (ii) the concept (Fr. *signifié*, 'the signified'). Mulder and Hervey (*op. cit.*, 27) here use the terms 'expression' and 'content'.

This present essay is not exclusively concerned with verbal communication or with *linguistic* signs. Just as we can think with words without actually speaking, we can think with visual and tactile images without using our eyes or actually touching anything. So I shall write of *sense-images* rather than sound images. The difficulty is to understand how the sense-image, with which we can play games in our imagination, is related to objects and events in the world out-there. The puzzles are of several kinds.

First there is the difficulty which in language appears as homonymy and synonymy. The words *hair* and *hare* in English are homonyms; they are identical as sound images. But they are quite different kinds of object and we do not confuse them as concepts, though when we make puns we can play games in our imagination with the identity of the two sound images. Punning incidentally is an extremely important feature of all forms of symbolic communication but especially perhaps in areas of social life which are the focus of taboo such as sex and religion. The puns may be visual as well as verbal. Cock, the bird, has been a metaphor for the human penis in all parts of Europe at least since the days of Classical Greece, so that visual images of cock-fighting and of cocks and hens may be heavily loaded with sexual implication. Comparably the innocent 'bunny' is baby-talk for much less innocent 'cunny (coney)' and the contemporary Playboy's 'bunny girls' have their ancestry in eighteenth-century 'cunny houses' (brothels).

Synonymy is the reverse process by which a single concept in the mind may be manifested in two entirely different sound-images even within the context of the same language. Thus, in English, *kill* is the same as *slay*, a *ship* is the same as a *vessel*. Here again there are non-verbal analogies for the verbal usage. In almost all religious systems the core theological idea, the most sacred and heavily tabooed concepts, can be represented by several alternative standardised symbols. For example in early Christianity the Cross, the Chi-Rho symbol (an anagram of the first two letters of the word 'Christos'), and the Fish were all equivalent symbols. The fish involved a verbal pun – the Greek letters of the word *i-ch-th-e-u-s* being read as 'Jesus Christ, God and Saviour'.

But the pattern is a general one. The very fact that names which are applied to the things and events of the external world are arbitrary conventions implies an ambiguity about the sense-images and conceptualisations which the appearance of these things evoke and about

18

the kinds of things which we use as representations of metaphysical ideas.

We meet here a second major difficulty. While some concepts originate as descriptions of objects and events in the external world, e.g. nouns such as *cow* or verbs such as *kill*, others (e.g. the distinction between *good* and *bad*) are generated in the mind without reference to particular things and events in the external world. Even so, by the use of signs and symbols, we can project these mentally generated concepts onto things and actions in the external world. For example, when we dress a bride in a veiled garment of white and a widow in a very similar veiled garment of black, we are using the opposition *white/black* to express not only *bride/widow* but also *good/bad* as well as a whole range of subsidiary harmonic metaphors such as *happy/sad, pure/contaminated*.

The mechanism by which these ambiguities of meaning creep into the system can be represented schematically by Fig 2.

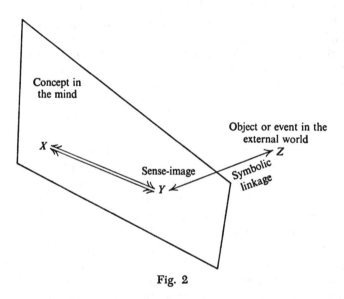

Fig. 2

The relationship between X – 'the concept in the mind' – and Y – 'the sense-image' – is intrinsic, they are two sides of the same penny, but the relation between Y – 'the sense-image' – and Z – 'the object in the external world' – is always arbitrary, at least to some extent.

From this it follows that, in my language, the linkage Z/Y is always symbolic (metaphoric). But that flat assertion must be qualified. In so far as the linkage Z/Y becomes stabilised by convention and habitual use, it is a sign.

19

Following Mulder and Hervey I have already made this same point at p. 13. If we distinguish a single man from a crowd of men and give him a name *John* that usage is symbolic, but when we use the word *pig* to denote all animals of a particular type wherever they occur, we are using the word pig as a sign. But what then are we doing if we apply the word *pig* to a policeman? Clearly symbolism is coming in again. We shall see later that this is by no means a trivial matter. It has a bearing on the anthropologist's understanding of magic. However the point I am making here is simply that the opposition *intrinsic / arbitrary* is not clear cut. Any arbitrary association which is used over and over again begins in the end to appear intrinsic.

At the risk of seeming tedious I want to pursue this matter of the basic arbitrariness of the linkage Z/Y rather further.

In the case of verbal language, the initial arbitrariness is obvious. The animal out-there which an Englishman calls *dog*, a Frenchman will call *chien*. The English word *dog* and the French word *chien* are arbitrary metaphors (symbols) for the same thing. By the same token the link between sound image and concept is palpably intrinsic. My English concept of dogginess is evoked by the word *dog* and *not* by the word *chien*. The word *dog* is part of *my* concept, *chien* is not. Because English is my mother tongue 'dog, the word' and 'dog, the internalised concept' seem to be inseparable.*

This feeling of identity between the things in the world and their names reaches very deep. In mythologies of all kinds including those

* Clearly this formulation begs a number of difficult questions. What happens, for example, to the sound-image/concept relationship in the case of individuals who are genuinely bilingual? And there are other difficulties. Mulder and Hervey (1972, 26–63) make an extremely intricate analysis of the problems surrounding the relationships between X, Y, and Z in Fig. 2 as they affect the words of a single spoken language, e.g. English. They claim to dispose of the sorts of ambiguity to which I have referred by describing the X of my diagram as 'a class of equivalent referents' and the Y of my diagram as 'a class of equivalent forms'. X and Y in combination are then a *sign* of Z. In the process Mulder and Hervey necessarily put great strain on their original definition of signs as 'signa with wholly fixed conventional denotation'. In any case, so far as I can judge, the Mulder and Hervey approach, which they call 'denotational sign-semantics', is inapplicable to problems of translation in which one 'language', either verbal or non-verbal, is being interpreted in another. And it is precisely interpretation of this latter sort which provided the subject matter of my present essay.

20

of the Australian Aborigines and the Judaeo-Christian Bible, the naming of animals and plants is a creative act which gives them independent existence.

But although you will have no difficulty about accepting the following rather obvious proposition as it applies to words: 'my concepts are linked to particular words in a particular language; things in the world are linked with different words in different languages', you may well be reluctant to transfer the argument to a non-verbal context.

Obviously the words *dog* and *chien* are different representations of the same thing, but surely my visual response to 'the thing, dog', my total sense-image of the creature, cannot be similarly subject to cultural conditioning? But are you really sure about this? How confident can we be that our perception of the world is independent of our social environment?

This is an issue which is a source of wide dispute among experienced anthropologists and psychologists and I am certainly not prepared to be dogmatic on the subject. But the artistic representation of common objects follows widely different conventions in different cultures and this seems significant. It is perfectly possible that every individual perceives his world to be what his or her cultural background suggests. Today most of the world is dominated by the 'realistic' images provided by our use of cameras. But it is self-deception if you imagine – as you probably do – that your eye 'naturally' perceives the world as it might appear in a photograph.

But let me go back for a moment to the proposition 'policemen are pigs'. The association is plainly arbitrary and therefore symbolic (metaphoric); to suppose that it is intrinsic and therefore in the nature of a metonymic sign would be an error. But, as we shall see, it is an important kind of error which all of us are inclined to make. It is one of the standard devices which we employ to mask the fact that nearly everything we say or do is full of ambiguity.

The diagram Fig. 2 helps to explain how the ambiguity arises in the first place. Suppose we start with Z as an example of the familiar farm animal known in English as *cow*. Then the appearance of this animal will generate in the mind of an English beholder both a visual image and a sound-image *cow*. These two versions of Y serve to classify the animal in question as a *cow* and not a *horse*, but X, 'the concept *cow* in the mind', is not equally attached to both visual image and sound-image and we can play mental games with either. In particular, we can attach particular attributes of the visual image to the sound image so as to provide a basis for new metaphors. Thus the English word *cow* is applied not only to the familiar farm animal but also to female whales, female elephants, female seals, female rhinoceroses, and even on occasion to female human beings.

21

These uses are all metaphors but the associations are not *wholly* arbitrary; elements of metonymy are involved as is shown by the fact that wherever the female of a species is described as a cow the male is described as a bull.

This may strike you as a silly childish example but it is the principle of the thing that you need to think about. Metaphoric (symbolic) and metonymic (sign) relationships are notionally distinct and, indeed, in our ordinary processes of communication we make some show of keeping them apart. We have to do so in order to avoid ambiguity. But the latent ambiguity is always there and there are many special but important situations – as in poetic and religious utterance for example – when we go to the opposite extreme. By code switching between symbols and signs we are able to persuade one another that metaphoric non-sense is really metonymic sense.

4. *Signals and indices*

Before I go further I need to elaborate somewhat the very brief distinction which I have already made between a *signal* and an *index* (above, p. 12). You should again keep a watch on Fig. 1 (p. 12).

Signal refers to any automatic trigger response mechanism. In nature, most signals are biological. Every natural species has become adapted by evolution to respond to its environment by a complex mesh of signals. To take a simple human example. If I do not drink for several hours on a hot day I become thirsty. 'Feeling thirsty' is a biological signal which triggers off a response. I look for something to drink.

The extent to which communication between adult human individuals is governed by true signals is not at all clear, but a mother's responses to the cries and smiles of her infant are certainly largely 'instinctive', and we do not shed our animal nature as we get older.

Two general characteristics of signals deserve particular attention:

(1) A signal is always part of a cause and effect sequence. It is first generated by a prior cause and then functions as a cause to generate a later effect.

(2) There is always a time lag between a signal and its consequence.

Human technical actions which alter the physical state of the world out-there (p. 9) closely resemble signals in this respect. The principal difference is that signals are 'automatic' in that they do *not* entail an *intentional response* on the part of the receiver, but they are *not fully mechanical* in that the effectiveness of the signal depends upon the sense response of the receiver which is not fully predictable. Technical actions on the other hand *are fully mechanical* and they entail an *initial intentional act* on the part of the sender (actor).

This point has an important bearing on anthropological theories of magic (see below, Section 6).

The contrast between signal and index is that between dynamics and statics. With a *signal,* one event causes another event; the signal itself is the message. With an *index,* the message-bearing entity is an indication of the past, present or future existence of a message. No cause and effect relationship is involved. However, all animals, including man, react to habitually used indices as if they were signals.

This important point can be illustrated by the classic example of Pavlov's dog. Food was regularly presented to the dog to the accompaniment of the ringing of a bell. The true biological signal for the dog was the smell of the food which elicited a response of salivation from the start. But the dog learned to associate the bell with the food. Thereafter the ringing of the bell elicited a response of salivation even if the food was not presented. The bell was an index for the presence of food, but was treated as a signal.

A great deal of normal human education consists of learning an inventory of indices, both natural and man-made; we learn what goes with what. But having learned our lesson, we make mental short cuts and behave like Pavlov's dog. For example, in reading these words you can, by an effort of will, notice the individual indices, the printed letters on the paper, but ordinarily you will treat the printed letterpress as a signalling apparatus which automatically generates information 'in your mind's eye'.

But this, you may think, spoils the whole argument. Earlier, in Section 2, I explicitly used the case of a sequence of letters of the alphabet which spell out a word as an example of 'a syntagmatic chain of signs'. But now I am saying that, in actual practice, when we engage in the operation of reading, we treat such 'syntagmatic chains of signs' as if they were signals. So what is the point of the jargon-loaded analysis anyway?

5. Transformations

The concluding paragraphs of Sections 3 and 4 may lead the cynical reader to conclude that I have only set up the elaborate discriminations proposed in Section 2 and Fig. 1 (p. 12) in order to demonstrate that they are inapplicable to practical situations. To some extent this is true! Jakobson, who first emphasised the importance of the polarity *metaphor/metonymy* made it clear from the start that in actual observable forms of discourse, either verbal or non-verbal, the two modes are always mixed up, though one may predominate over the other. The prototype of a general message-bearing system is not a line of type but the performance of an orchestra where harmony and melody work in combination.

Jakobson's insight has been developed by Lévi-Strauss to provide his celebrated technique of myth interpretation. The key point here is not just that metaphor and metonymy, paradigmatic association and syntagmatic chain, are combined, but that the 'meaning' depends upon *transformations* from one mode into the other and back again.

To see just what Lévi-Strauss is getting at you need to follow through some of his examples in detail. But the formal principles of the method are fairly straight forward. Lévi-Strauss first breaks up the syntagmatic chain of the total myth story into a sequence of episodes. He then assumes that each episode is a partial metaphoric transformation of every other. This implies that the story as a whole can be thought of as a palimpsest of superimposed (but incomplete) metaphoric transformations.

If we accept these assumptions, it follows that the analyst who seeks to decode the message embodied in the myth as a whole (as distinct from the surface messages that are presented by the stories in the individual episodes) must look for a pattern of structure (which is necessarily of a somewhat abstract kind) which is common to the whole set of metaphors. The final interpretation consists of reading this derived pattern as if it were a syntagmatic chain. The procedure involves a double switch from the metonymic mode to the metaphoric and back to the metonymic.

Lévi-Strauss has himself represented this process by a mathematical formula (Lévi-Strauss (1966 (c) 211–12) and his imitators P. and E. K. Maranda (1971, 24–5) have formalised the argument even further. The original version, as presented by Lévi-Strauss in 1955, has subsequently been revamped in many forms, but it is still the easiest to understand. It can be represented by the following schema:

(a) We start with a mythical story which is linear in form, one thing happening after another. The events occur in sequence, that is they form a 'syntagmatic chain', they are linked by metonymy.

(b) The analyst then notes that the story as a whole can be broken up into episodes A, B, C.:

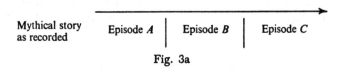

Fig. 3a

(c) Each of the episodes is then assumed to be a partial transformation of each of the others. So we rearrange the diagram to suggest that each of the sub-plots refers to simultaneous events, and 'add up' the result. In jargon, by the first of these steps the original 'syntagmatic chain' is transformed into a 'paradigmatic association' (metonymy is converted into metaphor), thus:

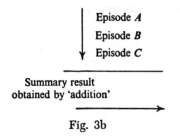

Fig. 3b

As compared with the details in the original episodes, the elements in the summary 'additive' story are abstract. It is a *structural* sequence which can best be represented as an algebraic equation of which each of the three original episodes was an imperfect manifestation. In jargon, this summation process amounts to the conversion of a 'paradigmatic association' into a 'syntagmatic chain'; metaphor is transformed into metonymy.

The basic principle involved is one which is common to all verbal expression and all ritual activity. Utterances are sequences in time; by their very nature they are syntagmatic chains of message-bearing elements. But most messages are synchronic, the

26

end is implicit in the beginning and vice versa. In interpreting a message we are always performing a feat comparable to that of translation from one language into another. We are, as it were, transposing the music from one key into another. The operation is a paradigmatic transformation.

When we are conveying messages by means of speech, the time interval between the beginning of the utterance and the end is so short that we are liable to forget that any time factor is involved at all. But correspondingly when we are trying to interpret ritual performances, we are liable to forget that events which are separated by a considerable interval of time may be part of the same message. I have mentioned one such case already; it is worth repeating. The Christian European customs by which brides are veiled and dressed in white and widows are veiled and dressed in black are both part of the same message. A bride is entering marriage, a widow is leaving it. The two customs are *logically* related. The reason we do not ordinarily see that they are logically related is because they are normally widely separated in time.

6. *Theories of magic and sorcery*

The performances which anthropologists classify as magic and sorcery provide excellent examples of the ambiguities I have been discussing and of the mixture of metonymic and metaphoric association which is characteristic of all modes of human communication.

The point that I want to get across to you in this section is that, with slight modification, the technique of analysis which Lévi-Strauss has applied so successfully to the interpretation of myth can be made to throw light on the logical mystifications of 'magic'.

Perhaps the first point to emphasise here is that ambiguity needs to be distinguished from error.

Earlier in this century anthropologists took it for granted that the manifest technological inferiority of primitive societies was the consequence of a general mental incapacity. Belief in magic was a symptom of this inferiority; it provided evidence that all primitive peoples are essentially childish and mentally confused.

The most generally accepted version of this theory was that of Sir James Frazer. In effect, Frazer held that 'expressive acts which purport to alter the state of the world by metaphysical means' are mistaken attempts at 'technical acts which alter the state of the world by physical means' (see above, p. 9). He declared that magic is 'bastard science'; its fundamental quality is erroneous belief about cause and effect. He then went on to distinguish two major types of the erroneous cause/effect nexus: (1) homoeopathic magic depending upon 'the law of similarity'; (2) contagious magic depending upon 'the law of contact'.

In so far as Frazer was wrong he was wrong in an interesting way. In the first place he assumed that the magician's mistake is to confuse expressive acts with technical acts, whereas the general consensus of most recent anthropologists is that what the magician usually does is to interpret an index as a signal, after the fashion of Pavlov's dog (see above, p. 24). On the other hand, as Jakobson noticed a long while back (Jakobson and Halle, 1956, pp. 80–1), Frazer's distinction between homoeopathic and contagious magic is essentially the same as that between metaphoric and metonymic association. Frazer's bastard scientist–magician plays around with iconic symbols (which depend upon metaphor) and signs (which depend upon metonymy).

Frazer's failure to distinguish between purported signals and purported technical acts is an error but it is not easy to demonstrate that it is error except by specific examples. The essence of the matter is that when magical performance is observed in action it is palpably quite different *in kind* from straightforward technical action. If a Sinhalese peasant wants to drive a stake into the ground, he takes a hammer and does just that; if he wants to stop a charging elephant he will (or should) stand stock still and recite a magical formula!

The essential difference between the two types of performance is that whereas the primitive *technician* is always in direct mechanical contact with the object which he seeks to change, the *magician* purports to change the state of the world by action at a distance. The argument about *sense-images* in Section 3 in relation to Fig. 2 (p. 19) is relevant here as is also the statement at p. 23 that *signals* are automatic trigger response mechanisms. In terms of Fig. 1 (p. 12) magical acts are *indices*; the magician treats them as *signals*.

This marginal slither by which technical action is confused with expressive action, and symbolic communication with signal communication, deserves the anthropologist's close attention.

In ordinary day-to-day affairs the only way that I can make things happen at a distance (in the absence of a mechanical connecting link) is to issue verbal (i.e. symbolic) instructions to a trained agent, human or animal. My verbal instruction is an expressive rather than a technical action, but if my agent responds to my message *as if it were a signal* (i.e. in an automatic fashion like Pavlov's dog) the existence of the intermediate linkage through the agent becomes irrelevant. The effect is *as if* I myself had performed a technical action at a distance.

Notice that in situations of this sort the effect of the verbal command will only be reliable if it conforms to a conventional habitual mode, i.e. if the symbolic instructions can be treated as signs (cf. p. 20). On the other hand if the verbal commands are of a *completely*, habitual kind, like the 'words' which are shouted by a sergeant major on a parade ground, it does not really matter what the words are; the noise itself can be treated as a signal. This is the general point. Where symbols are treated as signs, they can always very easily be perceived as signals.

It is thus very significant that the types of performance which anthropologists distinguish as magic invariably include a verbal (or sign language) component – the spell. It is the spell which is supposed to make the magical performance effective at a distance. This is a fallacy, but it is fallacy of a complicated sort.

Consider the following prototype example which might well come from Frazer:

'A sorcerer gains possession of a specimen of hair from the head of his intended victim X. The sorcerer destroys the hair to the accompaniment of spells and ritual. He predicts that, as a consequence, the victim X will suffer injury.'

What is the 'logic' of the sorcerer's fallacy?

In terms of Fig. 1 (p. 12) the connections are as follows: The sorcerer treats the hair growing on the head of X as a metonymic sign for X. He further assumes that if he destroys the sign he will damage X. This is perfectly 'reasonable'. In the expressions 'A stands for APPLE' and 'Crown stands for Kingship', A and Crown are metonymic signs for APPLE and KINGSHIP respectively. If you destroy the sign elements the residues are damaged: -PPLE and 'royal regalia without a headpiece' are indecipherable.

Now when the hair is growing on the head of the potential victim it is indeed a 'metonymic sign for X' in a genuine sense: the sign and the thing signified are contiguous; if the hair were destroyed, X would indeed be damaged. But by the time the hair has come into the sorcerer's possession the only continuing link with its origin is a verbal label 'this is the hair of X'. The label is now a metonymic sign for the *hair*, but the hair and X are separated; the link between the label and X is only metaphoric. In so far as a sense-image of X is generated in the mind of the sorcerer by the presence of the hair it entails the distinction, which was noted at p. 20), between proper names which are symbolic of the individual so named and category words, e.g. *pig*, *hair*, which are normally signs for the category indicated.

In summary, in terms of the specifications of Fig. 1 (p. 12) the sorcerer makes a triple error. He first mistakes a metaphoric symbol (i.e. the verbal label 'this is the hair of X') for a metonymic sign. He then goes on to treat the imputed sign as if it were a natural index, and finally he interprets the supposed natural index as a signal capable of triggering off automatic consequences at a distance.

You may perhaps think that this is a quite absurdly complicated, jargon-loaded way of describing what is quite obvious. I agree. But the mental associations of magical procedure are complicated and the logical errors are not nearly so self-evident as is sometimes thought to be the case. If you want to trace out just where the 'mistakes' occur you need to examine the chain of associations very carefully. Notice the similarities between my prototype anthropological example and the following more familiar situations:

Case 1. *Political sorcery*

In many parts of contemporary Latin America, Africa and Asia the normal method of changing the political regime is by military *coup*. In the great majority of instances the bloodshed involved is negligible. The insurrection is completed in a few hours and the leaders of the defeated government retire to a comfortable exile abroad. The form of such *coups* is quite standardised: it consists of a military assault on the Presidential Palace. In many cases it is later reported that the President himself was absent at the time. Newspaper and radio proclamations (spells) by the usurping military play a large part in the procedure.

The main difference between this kind of operation and that of my prototype sorcerer is that the intended victim's *hair* is replaced by the intended victim's *Presidential Palace*. The *coup* is an expressive rather than a technical act but in nine cases out of ten it achieves the desired result. You should not assume that magic and sorcery never work!

Case 2. *Techno-magic in the home*
You go into a room and notice on the wall a knob of a familiar kind. You take this to be a sign that the room is wired for electricity. Through long experience you have come to believe that you can treat the sign as a signal. You press the knob in the expectation that a light will come on somewhere in the room.

Most of the complex string of assumptions which lie at the back of your expectation could only be verified with considerable difficulty. It is habit rather than technical knowledge which persuades us to treat light switches as signals. And in point of fact, were it not for the absence of a verbal spell, it would be difficult to distinguish your light switching behaviour from an act of magic.

I am not suggesting that we *should* treat light switching as an act of magic, but only that, if Sir James Frazer had been consistent, *he* should have to have done so! The action is technical in intention and *may be* technical in its consequences, but the actual form of the action is expressive.

Because our day-to-day behaviour is full of logical ambiguities of this kind it is worth going to some trouble to get this business of signals, signs and symbols sorted out.

The distinctions are not mere pedantry. Admittedly the three types of communication dyad are constantly getting mixed up, but it is valuable to have the formal distinctions clear in your minds because it is by means of such distinctions and by refusing to admit that there is any ambiguity that we manage to perceive the world as we do.

If you doubt this, try to work out *in detail* just why you feel that the sorcerer's hocus-pocus with his intended victim's hair is 'magic' but that fiddling with an electric light switch is not.

7. The symbolic ordering of a man-made world: boundaries of social space and time

One crucial point here is that our internal perception of the world around us is greatly influenced by the verbal categories which we use to describe it. A modern urban street scene is wholly man-made and it is only because all the things in it carry individual names, i.e. symbolic labels, that we can recognise what they are. This is true of all human culture and of all human societies. We use language to cut up the visual continuum into meaningful objects and into persons filling distinguishable roles. But we also use language to tie the component elements together again, to put things and persons in relationship to one another. As my very first example about gift giving showed (p. 6), this double function of symbolic action applies to non-verbal as well as to verbal behaviour.

Much the same point is implicit in my contextual definition of *signs* (p. 14). All signs, and most symbols and signals, cohere together as sets. Meanings depend upon contrast. Red and Green lights mean Stop and Go, but only when they are contrasted one against the other and in their proper setting on a public highway. We recognise a light switch for what it is because we can distinguish it by shape and location from other knobs, such as door handles and window latches, which occur in the same general context. But if we saw the same object lying on the footpath we would not expect it to function as a light switch at all. One of my prototype sorcerer's mistakes is that he fails to make this distinction: he does not allow for the fact that the victim's hair, when separated from its proper context on the victim's head, changes its 'meaning'.

When we use symbols (either verbal or non-verbal) to distinguish one class of things or actions from another we are creating artificial boundaries in a field which is 'naturally' continuous. This notion of *boundary* needs to be thought about.

In principle, a boundary has no dimension. My garden abuts directly on that of my neighbour; the frontier of France abuts directly on that of Switzerland, and so on. But if the boundary is to be marked on the ground the marker itself will take up space. Neighbouring gardens tend to be separated by fences and ditches; national frontiers by

33

strips of 'no man's land'. It is the nature of such markers of boundaries that they are ambiguous in implication and a source of conflict and anxiety.

The principle that all boundaries are *artificial* interruptions to what is naturally continuous, and that the ambiguity, which is implicit in the boundary as such, is a source of anxiety, applies to time as well as to space.

The biological time-flow of physical experience is continuous; we simply get older and older 'all the time'. But in order to give a dimension to this time of experience we have to devise clocks and calendars which will break up the continuum into segments – seconds, minutes, hours, days, weeks. Each segment has duration, but notionally the intervals between the segments, like the bar lines on a musical score, have no duration. However, when we come to convert this notional time into social time by acting it out, each 'interval of no duration' itself takes up time.

For example, at the level of concept, the change of status from 'unmarried' to 'married' is simply a switch of categories, but at the level of action the switching calls for a ritual, a crossing of social frontiers which takes place in 'no man's time'.

This is a very simple example, but the general analogy between the segmentation of social space and the segmentation of social time has much wider application. Boundaries of social space appear in many other contexts besides those of property ownership and national frontiers; in particular they are involved in the various human contrivances by which we distinguish domesticated areas from wild areas, town from country, sacred precincts from secular dwellings, and so on. A comparable generality applies to the boundaries of social time.

We can see this most easily in the way we segment our normal activities. Each working week which progresses in a normal way from Monday to Saturday is separated from the next by a Sunday, an abnormal holiday (holy day), the basic characteristic of which is that nothing happens. And so also with each twenty-four hour day of ordinary life; periods of normal working activity are separated by intervals of 'timelessness' which somehow 'don't count', but are in fact devoted to eating or sleeping.

The same principle applies to the individual's progress through the totality of his (her) socially recognised existence. He (she) moves from one social status to another in a series of discontinuous jumps – child to adult, unmarried to married, living to dead, sick to healthy. The occupancy of each status constitutes a period of social time of social duration, but the ritual which marks the transition – puberty rite, wedding, funeral, healing ritual – is an interval of social timelessness.

This general discussion of space and time boundaries implies an-

other series of fundamental metaphoric equivalences, namely:
normal/abnormal::time bound/timeless::clear-cut categories/am-
biguous categories::at the centre/at the edge:secular/sacred.
A boundary separates two zones of social space-time which are *normal,
time-bound, clear-cut, central, secular,* but the spatial and temporal
markers which actually serve as boundaries are themselves *abnormal,
timeless, ambiguous, at the edge, sacred.*

But why should the 'sacred' be 'abnormal, timeless, ambiguous, at
the edge'? Perhaps my Euler diagram (Fig. 4) may help? There is
always some uncertainty about just where the edge of Category *A*
turns into the edge of Category not-*A*. Whenever we make category
distinctions within a unified field, either spatial or temporal, it is the
boundaries that matter; we concentrate our attention on the differences
not the similarities, and this makes us feel that the markers of such

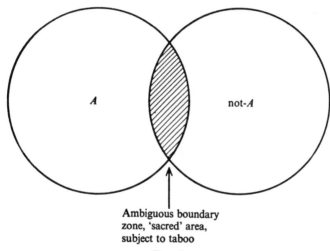

Ambiguous boundary
zone, 'sacred' area,
subject to taboo

Fig. 4

boundaries are of special value, 'sacred', 'taboo'. (Cf. Leach (1964).)

The crossing of frontiers and thresholds is always hedged about with
ritual, so also is the transition from one social status to another.

I shall be discussing the psychological roots of these cultural universals and the various particular patterns in which the general principles can be observed in later sections (see especially Sections 13(d),
16, 17). Here I only want to make two points. The first is that, in all
human societies, the great majority of ceremonial occasions are 'rites
of transition', which mark the crossing of boundaries between one social
category and another: puberty ceremonies, weddings, funerals, initi-
ation rites of all kinds are the most obvious examples.

Secondly I would emphasise that this whole process of carving up

35

the external world into named categories and then arranging the categories to suit our social convenience depends upon the fact that, although our ability to alter the external environment is very limited, we have a virtually unrestricted capacity for playing games with the internalised version of the environment which we carry in our heads. This point was made earlier (Section 3) in the discussion of sense-images, but needs further elaboration.

8. *The material representation of abstract ideas: ritual condensation*

It is high time that I began to persuade you that the highly abstract, formalistic, arguments that I have so far presented have some practical application when it comes to analysing the sort of ethnographic evidence with which social anthropologists regularly have to deal. In this section I shall make a start in that direction.

In Section 3 the point has already been made that while many concepts are the mental aspects of sense-images which are, in turn, a culturally determined response to objects and events in the external world, the sequence often goes the other way; that is to say we may generate abstract ideas in our heads (e.g. the opposition good/bad) and then give these abstractions manifest form by projecting them onto the external world, e.g. good/bad becomes white/black.

This is a very important part of normal thinking and calculation. By converting ideas, products of the mind (mentifacts), into material objects 'out-there', we give them relative permanence, and in that permanent material form we can subject them to technical operations which are beyond the capacity of the mind acting by itself. It is the difference between carrying out mathematical calculations 'in your head' and working things out with pencil and paper or on a calculating machine.

For anthropologists the most important area where this kind of material symbolisation is in evidence is in religious ritual. All metaphysical entities start out as inchoate concepts in the mind; if we are to think clearly about the ideas which are represented by words such as 'god' and 'spirit' we have to externalise them. We do this in two ways: (i) by telling stories (myths) in which the metaphysical ideas are represented by the activities of supernatural beings, magnified non-natural men and animals; (ii) by creating special material objects, buildings and spaces which serve as representations of the metaphysical ideas and their mental environment. Clearly, (i) and (ii) are interdependent; each is a metaphor for the other.

To take a case in point, the extremely difficult idea of 'communion with God' is represented in Christian mythology by the New Testament story of the Last Supper. This story is given material representation in a specially designed environment at the altar rails of the church every time there is a performance of the communion service (mass) in any of its multifarious forms.

This exemplifies a general process common to all religious behaviour in all human societies, but it is full of paradox and is a constant source of confused anxiety even for those who participate in the proceedings. When ritual objects (a crucifix, a portrait of the child Jesus, the bread and wine of the communion service) serve as material representations of divinity *in a ritual context*, they are infected by the aura of sanctity which initially belongs only to the metaphysical concept in the mind. But the objects continue to exist even when the ritual which first generated their sanctity is finished. It may then become an issue of theological dispute as to whether the sanctity which belongs to the objects in their ritual context still persists even in a non-ritual context.

At the time of the Reformation, Protestant Christians accused Catholic Christians of idolatry because of their reverence for the relics and images of saints and because of the 'reservation' of the bread and wine of the Mass.

In contrast, when Christian missionaries encounter a 'primitive' religion in which the shrines are constructed *ad hoc* and abandoned as soon as the ritual is over, they are inclined to treat this as a symptom of theological triviality! This is because Protestant Christians and Catholic Christians alike all share a cultural assumption that religious ritual calls for a permanent, specially designed, sacred environment – a church building.

The linguistic and proto-linguistic problems underlying such behaviour were discussed briefly in Section 3 and they are already implicit in Section 2 (p. 14) where I distinguish between *sign* and *symbol* in terms of 'context'. The concept of 'context', like the expression 'semiotic system' used by certain other authors (Barthes (1967); Mulder and Hervey (1972)), is, I am afraid, excessively vague but can be explained by example. In Fig. 2 (p. 19) it is clear that the overall relationship between Z – 'the object or event in the external world' and X – 'the concept in the mind' is one of *meaning*, but it is also clear that it is meaning of a different sort from that which appears in tautologous formulae such as '$2 \times 2 = 4$' where all the entities are abstract, or 'smoke is a natural index of fire' where the representations *smoke* and *fire* are both entities in the external world. In these two examples the items which are brought into relation, the numerals in the one case, the smoke and fire in the other, belong to the same context. In contrast, in Fig. 2 a transformation takes place such that an observable entity Z is converted into an abstraction X, or vice versa. X and Z belong to different contexts.

Let me remind you once again of that tedious Fig. 1 (p. 12) and the

38

connected definitions. The argument there was that where the entities A and B of the communication dyad are from the same context we are dealing with *signs* and *natural indices* and the relations are mainly *metonymic*, but that when A and B come from different contexts we are dealing with *symbols* and the relations are mainly *metaphoric*.

This brings us back to the point I made earlier in Section 6 when discussing light switches and sorcerers. The essence of the matter is that, with *symbolism* (metaphor), as distinct from *signals*, *natural indices* and *signs*, we use our human imagination to associate together two entities, or sets of entities, either material or abstract, which ordinarily belong to quite different contexts. Thus:

(1) 'the lion is a beast' is a statement referring to a normal non-human context 'in Nature';
(2) 'the king is the most powerful man in the state' is a statement referring to a normal human context 'in Society';
(3) 'the lion is the king of beasts' is a symbolic (metaphoric) statement. It acquires meaning by mixing the two contexts 'in the mind'.

A metaphoric mixing of contexts of this general sort is characteristic of all material forms of religious expression. Thus:

(1) 'The god Śiva is a source of divine potency' is a statement in a metaphysical context.
(2) 'The penis is a source of animal potency' is a statement in the context of functional biology.
(3) 'The *lingam* is a carved object shaped like a penis' is a statement in the context of material physics, which involves an iconic relationship between *lingam* and penis.
(4) The familiar Hindu assertion that 'the *lingam* is the god Śiva' then acquires meaning by mixing together the contexts of (1), (2) and (3) 'in the mind'.

You must not get the idea that that is all that can be said on the matter, but wherever the idea of deity is represented by a material object – a *lingam*, a cross, an altar, an 'idol', a sacred relic, a sacred book, a temple – metaphoric/metonymic transformations are involved, and condensation of this kind comes into it somewhere along the line. Very often the symbolic equations will be highly obscure but, regardless of whether the devotees understand the system or not, there will always be method in their madness. Provided you go about things in a systematic way, it should always be possible, up to a point, to decipher the coding that is involved. And indeed that is one of the principal tasks of social anthropology. The only justification for introducing my metaphoric/metonymic jargon into this essay is that it makes such partial decoding possible.

A classic example of this kind of problem is provided by the case of

Australian totemism, the interpretation of which has been a bone of contention among anthropologists ever since the ethnographic facts first began to be reported around the middle of the last century. Totemism appears to entail the 'worship' of species of plants and animals. This seems absurd. By what chain of reasoning could such behaviour come to seem sensible?

I suggest that from the point of view of a participant member of an Australian Aborigine totemic group the metaphoric condensations are roughly as follows:

(1) '*We* are all members of one social group because we are descended from a common ancestor' is initially an idea 'in the mind'.

(2) Similarly, '*they* are all members of one social group because they are descended from a common ancestor' is initially an idea 'in the mind'.

(3) 'These white birds are Eaglehawks; those black birds are Crows' are classificatory statements belonging to the context of non-human Nature.

(4) ' "We" differ from "they" as "Eaglehawks" differ from "Crows" ' is a simple metaphor.

(5) 'We are Eaglehawks because our first ancestor was an Eaglehawk; they are Crows because their first ancestor was a Crow' is a 'logical' consequence of collapsing 1, 2, 3 and 4.

Pursued thus far, the ideology of totemism is primarily a system of social classification. Social groups in human society are recognised for what they are by using the analogy 'the difference between human groups is like the difference between animal species'. But this aspect of the matter, which has been elaborated by Lévi-Strauss (1962), leaves out of account the religious attitudes involved. These call for a further set of condensations:

(6) 'We and they live in time-bound ordinary life; events happen one after another; all living things are destined to die' is a statement expressing normal experience.

(7) 'If we were not destined to die, events would not happen one after another; happenings would be timeless, as in a dream' is a logical derivation from (6) which implies the following oppositions:

$$\frac{\text{Normal time}}{\text{Dream time}} : \frac{\text{Beginning} \rightarrow \text{End}}{\text{Beginning} = \text{End}} : \frac{\text{Life} \rightarrow \text{Death}}{\text{Life} = \text{Death}} :$$

$$\frac{\text{Ancestors no longer exist}}{\text{Ancestors still exist}} : \frac{\text{We are mortal (Men)}}{\text{Ancestors are immortal (Gods)}}$$

(8) 'In adopting ritual attitudes towards the species Eaglehawk and the species Crow, we and they are showing reverence to our an-

cestors, who are Gods, who exist now in dreamtime' is a condensation of 5, 6 and 7.

The first recorded ethnographic descriptions of Australian totemism
were, as it happens, very similar to the last formula (8).

Although I believe that all varieties of religious ritual involve comparable multiple condensations, I would hasten to add that any step by
step decoding procedure such as I have given above gives a quite misleading impression of what really goes on in the communication process.

Because the analysis is bound to take a verbal metonymic form, with
one thing following after another, the overall impression is one of enormous complexity and total disjointedness. But what actually *happens*
is that the participants in a ritual are sharing communicative experiences through many different sensory channels simultaneously;
they are acting out an ordered sequence of metaphoric events within
a territorial space which has itself been ordered to provide a metaphoric context for the play acting. Verbal, musical, choreographic, and
visual–aesthetic 'dimensions' are all likely to form components of the
total message. When we take part in such a ritual we pick up all these
messages at the same time and condense them into a single experience
which we describe as 'attending a wedding', or 'attending a funeral',
and so on. But the analyst must take each dimension by itself, one at a
time, and it then becomes almost impossible to give a really *convincing*
account of how the different superimposed dimensions fit together to
produce a single combined message.

I made much the same point in Section 5 when I pointed out that
because the telling of a myth or the performance of a ritual takes time,
it is not easy to appreciate that episodes which appear near the beginning may be directly related to episodes which appear near the end.
But now I want to stress the added complication that, although the
receiver of a ritual message is picking up information through a variety
of different sensory channels simultaneously, all these different sen-
sations add up to just one 'message'.

It is condensations and associations of these kinds that I have in
mind when I say that, up to a point, a performance of orchestral music
provides a helpful prototype model of what goes on in any kind of
ritual sequence.

9. *Orchestral performance as a metaphor for ritual sequence*

Lévi-Strauss, who has contributed so much to our understanding of meta-linguistic modes of communication, constantly refers to the structural similarity between myth and music. In a celebrated and characteristically opaque statement he has declared that 'the myth and the musical work are like conductors of an orchestra, whose audience becomes the silent performers' (Lévi-Strauss, 1970, 17). What on earth can he be talking about?!

At one level he is simply making the point that the senders and receivers of messages which are contained in cultural communication are very often the same people. When we participate in ritual we 'say' things to ourselves. But the same sequence of behaviours may mean different things to different people. In general, all Christian sects share the same myths and engage in the same rites, but they disagree passionately about what they mean.

But there is much more to Lévi-Strauss's very complicated musical metaphor than that. A simplified version may help to bring the whole of the foregoing discursive argument into focus.

First let me remind you of the equivalences spelled out at the very end of Section 2. Approximately, though not exactly, Symbol/Sign = Metaphor/Metonymy = Paradigmatic association/Syntagmatic chain = Harmony/Melody. In music, the elements of melody (the individual notes and phrases played in succession) are linked together by metonymy; the relations of harmony, which allow for the transposition of a melodic phrase from one instrument to another, are those of metaphor.

Second, bear in mind the overall purpose of this enquiry. We are trying to understand the process by which information is transmitted between human beings by verbal and non-verbal means in combination. In such an analysis we necessarily start by distinguishing the variety of channels of communication through which messages may flow and the variety of types of association by which message elements may be combined. But we must not forget that, at the end of the day, the sense impressions which reach the receiver, however complex their structure or however ambiguous and polysemic their implication, are all apprehended as a *single* message. Moreover the message as a whole, although it takes time to transmit, has a unity. The end is implicit in the beginning; the beginning presupposes the end. Lévi-Strauss has remarked that myth and music are both 'machines for the suppression of time'; the same might be said of ritual sequence in general.

So here is my analogy, which is a modification of that used by Lévi-Strauss.

When an orchestra performs, let us say, a Beethoven Symphony the communication system that is involved is clearly highly complex. It includes the following elements:

(1) There is the 'full orchestra score', prepared originally by Beethoven himself but subsequently much edited. This was a material expression of music 'heard' as sense-images in Beethoven's 'mind' and then transformed into a complex pattern of marks on paper. The written text of the music is on two axes:.

   (i) Horizontally the text reads lineally and sequentially from left to right and describes melodic phrases (tunes) peculiar to particular instruments.

   (ii) Vertically the text is to be read synchronically; it describes harmonic combinations of sound which are to be produced by different kinds of instrument producing chords and phrases simultaneously. Besides these two main axes the full score contains various instructions to the conductor about pace and mood which are intended to aid his interpretation.

The music as a whole is divided into 'movements' which are related to each other by aesthetic rather than manifest association. Theme elements from one movement are likely to appear in direct or transposed form in another. For the musically sensitive listener, each phrase, each movement, and the symphony as a whole, form a system of interconnected unities. The whole performance may take an hour but the message is transmitted as if everything happened simultaneously.

(2) Besides the complete score which records the music as a whole there are further separate score sheets for each group of instruments in the orchestra – flutes, oboes, first violin, second violin, horns, drums, etc., etc. Each of these scores is in the 'melodic' linear form of (i) above. But the noise produced by a single instrument playing by itself makes no musical sense. It is only when the instruments play in combination according to the commands of the conductor which are delivered in gesture language that meaningful music results.

(3) Each instrumentalist reads his score with his eyes. But he then

44

transforms the instructions provided by the written text into complex movements of the arms, fingers, lips, etc. in accordance with the techniques required by the particular instrument in question.

(4) The conductor operates similarly but he has to read the full orchestra score all at once. He has to think in several dimensions simultaneously maintaining both the linear flow of the music over-all as a diachronic sequence, and the harmonic combinations of the different instrumentalists by ensuring that they all 'keep time with one another'.

(5) The combination of noises which is produced as a result of this complex of visual and manual operations issues from the orchestra as a pattern of sound waves. In this shape it eventually reaches the ears of individual members of the audience where it is transformed back into a mental impression of music which is (hopefully) not entirely different from the 'message' which Beethoven intended to transmit in the first place.

This example can serve as a general paradigm of ritual process in several ways. First the audience of an orchestra are interested in what all the instrumentalists and the conductor do in combination. The meaning of the music is not to be found in the 'tunes' uttered by individual instruments but in the combination of such tunes, in their mutual relations, and in the way particular patterns of sound are transformed into different but related shapes.

And so it is with expressive performances of all kinds. For analytical purposes it may be useful to distinguish (as I have done) at least three kinds of elements in any human message-bearing system, namely, signal, sign and symbol, but in practical cases there is always confusion. Signs are converted into symbols, symbols into signs, signs and symbols both masquerade as signals and so on.

But notice also the contrary aspect of the model. In ordinary culturally defined ritual performance there is no 'composer' other than the mythological ancestors. The proceedings follow an ordered pattern which has been established by tradition – 'this is our custom'. There *is* usually a 'conductor', a master of ceremonies, a chief priest, a central protagonist, whose actions provide the temporal markers for everyone else. But there is no separate audience of listeners. The performers and the listeners are the same people. We engage in rituals in order to transmit collective messages to ourselves.

10. *The physiological basis of sign/symbol sets*

I have just remarked that 'signs and signals both masquerade as signals'. I gave an example in Section 4 when referring to Pavlov's dog, but I now want to take the point rather further.

Since signals are part of our animal nature they are clearly the most basic components in our communication system. Cultural devices, however complex, must always be built on biological foundations. But although some of the signalling mechanisms manifested in physical reactions of the human body are fairly obvious, there is considerable controversy about others, and about where 'instinct' ends and 'culture' begins.

Smiling, weeping, laughing are universally part of the inventory of infant behaviour. Kissing seems to be a modification of suckling. Penile erection is a male adult reaction to erotic stimulus of various kinds. Eye and eyelid movements signal recognition. Anger, fear, shame are descriptions of 'emotions' which are a psychological reflex of physical reactions which are probably common to the whole species.

In appropriate circumstances nearly all such automatic reactions may be used to convey culturally recognised messages. For example, in English convention weeping 'means' sorrow, laughter 'means' joy, a kiss 'means' love. But these conscious associations are not human universals and sometimes the symbol/sign meaning of an action can be completely divorced from the signal response to which it refers.

For example, formalised weeping very frequently forms part of the correct behaviour of mourners at a funeral. But the official mourners are not necessarily the individuals whom one might expect to be emotionally affected. Indeed, in some cases 'those who weep' are simply hired professionals quite unrelated to the deceased. Also, weeping and laughter may form part of the same context; at a Chinese wedding the kin of the bride are expected to indicate their loss by tears while the kin of the bridegroom indicate their joy by laughter.

A further complication here is that the exhibition of emotion is commonly subject to the most stringent taboos so that what is shown

47

to be the case may be quite different from what is felt. Moreover, what is felt may itself be ambiguous.

A striking example of this point is provided by *Rivers of Sand*, a recent ethnographic film of the Hamar of Ethiopia made by Robert Gardner. The main theme of the film is the exaggerated economic subjection of married women to their husbands. The subjection is given symbolic expression when, on various ritual occasions, young men whip their potential wives with great severity. The film gives examples of this whipping but it is quite evident that a strong sado-masochistic erotic element is involved. The girls visibly experience excitement in their docile submission to brutality.

This same kind of ambiguity applies to all physical responses. All human beings have the same kinds of muscles and the same kind of physiology. The consequent limb movements and grimaces which we can make intentionally are a residue of our pre-human evolutionary past when they were only made unintentionally. Whenever we use parts of the body to make voluntary gestures we necessarily have to make do with what we have got. Our possible movements are limited by our biological endowment so that up to a point every controlled movement (or lack of movement) is masquerading as an automatic biological response, a natural signal. And clearly every such movement, or lack of movement, *may* be credited with meaning. But this is not always the case; nor is the attributed meaning always the same.

For example, head movements often indicate 'assent' or 'denial'. But where an Englishman would nod his head forward, some Asians would throw their head back, while others would rock the head from side to side on a horizontal axis.

In this case all that can be said is that if there is a particular body gesture which means 'yes' there will always be some other more or less similar gesture which means 'no' (e.g. in English head movements: 'nodding' = yes; 'shaking' = no). But there are two wider generalisations which may be derived from the biological roots of potential body symbolism.

First, any muscle which can be contracted can also be relaxed; *all* movements are potentially binary; if I step forward I can also step back.

Second, the human body is imperfectly symmetrical. Taking the navel as centre, the arms 'match' the legs, the genitals 'match' the head, the left side 'matches' the right side. But these paired dyads are contrasted, not identical; I cannot put a right-handed glove on my left hand. The upper and lower parts of the body, the right and left side are thus specially suited for the representation of related but contrary ideas – e.g. *good/bad*; and so indeed it is, but not universally.

48

All this illustrates once again the central principle to which I keep on returning. *The indices in non-verbal communication systems, like the sound elements in spoken language, do not have meaning as isolates but only as members of sets. A sign or symbol only acquires meaning when it is discriminated from some other contrary sign or symbol.*

11. *Mapping: time and space as reciprocal representations*

One example of the general principle formulated at the end of Section 10 is an ordinary ordnance survey map.

In the terminology of Section 2 the map as a whole is an *icon*. It serves as a metaphoric description of the terrain and employs various devices of 'planned similarity', e.g. a 'bend in a road' corresponds to a 'bend in a line' on the map.

However a map of this kind is also a metaphoric representation of time. I can use it to work out itineraries, not only so that I have a list of the places that I must pass through in order to get from locality A to locality B but also so that I can estimate the time interval that I shall experience in the process of doing so.

In these respects each map must be viewed as a unity, but the map as a whole can only be interpreted if we first make ourselves familiar with the mutual significance of several dozen conventional signs which are arranged on the paper in patterns.

All this is a complex process and, bearing in mind that the individual signs are *not* arranged in linear sequence like the individual letters on the typeface you are now reading, or the notes on a musical score, it may seem rather remarkable that we can read a map at all. Yet the making and reading of two dimensional maps is almost universal among mankind whereas the reading and writing of linear scripts is a special accomplishment associated with a high level of social and technical sophistication.

The explanation of this seeming paradox lies in what has already been said in Section 7. Our whole social environment is map-like.

Whenever human beings construct a dwelling or lay out a settlement they do so in a geometrically ordered way. This seems to be as 'natural' to Man as his capacity for language. We *need* order in our surroundings.

This contrast between human Culture and Nature is very striking. Visible, wild, Nature is a jumble of random curves; it contains no straight lines and few regular geometrical shapes of any kind. But the tamed, man-made world of Culture is full of straight lines, rectangles, triangles, circles and so on.

It follows that the contrast between 'man-made "geometrical"

51

topography' and 'random natural topography' is itself a metonymic sign for the wider general contrast between Culture and Nature.

But the ordering of human culture is not simply a static topographical arrangement of man-made things, it is also a dynamic progression of segmented, time-bound, events, each of which is associated with a particular location in man-made space. Sleeping, washing, cooking, eating, working . . . are not only socially determined activities which take place at different times in a predictable order, they are activities performed in different localities which are related to each other in predictable sets. Each locality has a specific function which is protected by taboo; defecation in the kitchen is just as sacrilegious as cooking in the bathroom.

All this ties in with a number of the jargon-loaded discriminations which were made earlier.

At the beginning of Section 2, I distinguished *technical actions* (things done) from *expressive actions* (things said) and later, in Sections 4 and 6, when distinguishing *signal* from *index*, I noted that:

(a) *indices* are static; *signals* dynamic

(b) *signals* always involve cause and effect sequences in time, whereas *indices*, although they may take time to transmit, relate to messages which have no time dimension

(c) *magical performances* are indices masquerading as signals, in that they purport to be automatic cause and effect mechanisms.

But technical actions are likewise 'cause and effect sequences in time' and, as became clear in my discussion of Frazer's view of magic (Section 6), it is very easy to mistake an expressive magical performance, masquerading as a signal, for a purported technical action.

From this certain generalisations follow. The material topographical features (both man-made and natural) of the space within which ritual performances take place – i.e. buildings, paths, forests, rivers, bridges etc. – constitute a set of *indices* for such metaphysical discriminations as this world/other world, secular/sacred, low status/high status, normal/abnormal, living/dead, impotent/potent.

But the ritual performances themselves, being dynamic, are to be regarded as *signals* which automatically trigger off a change in the (metaphysical) state of the world.

In such performances the movement of individuals from one physical locality to another and the sequence in which such movements are accomplished are themselves part of the message; they are direct representations of 'changes in metaphysical position'.

Sequences can form part of the message in more ways than one but one obvious possibility is for sequence to be transformed into hierarchy, e.g. the leader of a procession is the leader in social rank order. However the metaphors of rank order are not always that simple.

12. *Rank order and orientation*

Any classification in which the classes are spelled out in sequence 1, 2, 3 . . . implies a potential ranking of the categories. First Class is not just different from Second Class, it is better.

We make qualitative distinctions of this kind on all sorts of grounds. X may differ from Y because it is 'better', 'bigger', 'faster', 'more expensive', 'more powerful', 'older', etc., etc. In such qualitative statements it may be difficult to decide where description ends and symbolic statement begins. If an anthropologist in New Guinea is told 'so-and-so is a big man' should he infer that 'so-and-so' is physically large and powerful or that he is a political leader, or both?

Qualitative metaphors are not human universals but, as between one cultural context and another, they are often very similar. The politically influential are 'superior', and therefore sit 'higher up'. But sitting 'higher up' may mean that the chair is on a raised dais, or it may mean that the chair is at one end of the table rather than another.

Etiquette may require that persons of 'lower' status prostrate themselves on the ground or bow the head in the presence of their 'superiors', but equally it may require that the inferiors stand up while the superiors sit down. Such permutations are all using the same set of up/down discriminations to serve as metaphors, but the patterning of the total system is not predictable in advance. Likewise the order in which individuals move in ceremonial procession almost always carries implication about their relative status, but in some processions the persons of highest status are at the front and in others they are at the back.

Built into such codings is an awareness of the symmetries and asymmetries of the human body and of topographical space. My left hand is both like and unlike my right hand; the 'fixed' north/south axis of the external world is both like and unlike the 'shifting' east/west axis which provides the pathway of the heavenly bodies. In the metaphorical transformation of such awareness, astronomy and human destiny and the ordering of society become part of a single complex.

If the natural terrain fails to provide an obvious focus to which the whole may be anchored, culture can readily produce a substitute.

53

For example, most of Mongolia is a featureless plain; the round felt tents of the inhabitants are mobile structures, easily dismantled. Traditionally each tent was precisely oriented with the entrance towards the south. The space within the tent was divided into a complex grid, east/west, north/south in such a way that exactly predictable social, technical or ritual activities were carried out in each part of the tent's volumetric space.

The rigidity of this pattern by which the rank and status and sex of an individual exactly determined the space he or she might occupy was noted by European travellers even in the thirteenth century and with modifications the system still operates even today under a Soviet regime. If we ask: 'But why should people behave like this?' the answer may be that all human beings have a deep psychological need for the sense of security which comes from knowing where you are. But 'knowing where you are' is a matter of recognising social as well as territorial position.

So we make maps of social space by using territorial space as a model. In such usages the more featureless the context of actual territorial space, the more rigid and artificial the model has to be.

The orientation symbolism which has received most attention from a comparative point of view is that by which the left hand is 'sinister', 'gauche' (abnormal in some sense, evil, dirty, but also perhaps 'sacred') while the right hand is 'right', 'correct', 'normal', 'secular' (see Needham, 1973). Discriminations of this sort are certainly very common but oversimplified generalisations on the subject need to be treated with caution. The political Left only appears 'sinister' if your own political inclinations are on the Right. There are still countries, such as my own, where it is right to drive on the left!

13. *Examples of binary coding*

In Section 2 I assumed that 'all the various non-verbal dimensions of culture . . . are organised in patterned sets so as to incorporate coded information. . .' (p. 10) and I have repeatedly implied a close analogy between, for example, the cultural conventions governing the wearing of clothes and the grammatical and phonological rules governing the pattern of speech utterances. In particular I have reiterated the *leitmotif* which I spelled out at the end of Section 10: 'a sign or symbol only acquires meaning when it is discriminated from some other contrary sign or symbol' and 'they do not have meaning as isolates but only as members of sets'.

I shall now consider some practical, though very cursory and superficial, examples of this formula in rather greater detail. But let me be clear; these examples are intended just as rough illustrations of what I have been talking about. Read again what I said about ethnographic evidence in my introduction. If you want to understand the real force of the argument you must dig up further more complicated examples for yourself.

(a) *Costume*

Taken out of context, items of clothing have no 'meaning'; they can be stacked away in a drawer like the individual letters which a typographer uses to make up his typeface but, when put together in sets to form a uniform, they form distinctive markers of specified social roles in specified social contexts. Male and female, infant, child and adult, master and servant, bride and widow, soldier, policeman, high court judge, are all immediately recognisable by the clothing they wear.

The majority of such roles are impermanent and, as we saw in Section 7, our progression from social status to social status proceeds by a series of discontinuous jumps. Very frequently we mark such changes of status by changes of dress. The way such changes are carried through is very relevant to my theme.

The general theory of rites of transition (*rites de passage*) which

55

mark the movement of individuals across social boundaries will be discussed below in Section 17. Here I only want to make the point that, at the beginning of such a rite, *all* the participants nearly always 'dress up for the occasion', that is to say they first adopt abnormal dress so that the social boundaries ('the relevant context') can be seen to exist. Thereafter, in the course of the proceedings, the *initiates* who are undergoing a change of status take off or put on special costumes to mark their change of status.

If this kind of fancy dress behaviour is to convey meaningful information, the costumes in question must be highly standardised and easily recognised. But once a particular uniform comes to be habitually associated with a particular rite or with a particular social office associated with that rite, then any characteristic part of the uniform may be used as a metonymic sign for the rite or office.

I have mentioned some examples already: 'A crown stands for a King', 'A mitre stands for a Bishop'. But when a costume labels the wearer, it not only says what he is, it also, by implication, says what he is not. When costumes are very similar but contrasted in a single particular, this binary quality becomes explicit – bride:widow::white:black.

Here is a more trivial example of the same usage which shows up the logical principle involved.

Until very recently it was common practice in certain sections of contemporary English society to mark invitation cards for an evening dinner party with one or other of three formality indicators. 'White Tie' meant 'Very Formal'. Males were expected to wear a stiff-fronted white shirt, white tie and black tail coat, though persons of eminence such as bishops might wear even more splendid attire. 'Black Tie' meant 'Semi-Formal'. Males were expected to wear a dinner jacket (tuxedo), with soft shirt and bow tie of some sort. This could never be white, but need not be black! 'Informal Dress' meant what it says.

The invitation cards thus managed to convey a substantial amount of socially significant information by very economical means. All the information is incorporated into the two discriminations:

(i) WHITE/not WHITE (ii) BOW TIE/not BOW TIE

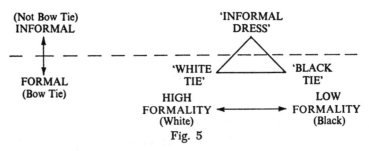

Fig. 5

Such message systems operate as follows. We first of all need to know in advance what parameters are involved, i.e. what the message is about. In this case it is about 'formality'.

If we then have two indices, P and Q, which form part of a set, we can first ask ourselves: In respect of the given parameter, do P and Q both fall into the same category or not? There are two possible answers: either $P = Q$ or $P \neq Q$.

If $P \neq Q$ we can then go on to ask some other question, e.g.: In respect of the given parameter, is P greater than Q or not? Again there are only two possible answers. And so on.

Digital computers operate on precisely this principle. All information is processed by asking strings of questions to which there are only two possible answers: YES/NO. If you have sufficient time and machinery you can solve almost any 'logical' problem by number crunching procedures of this kind.

Human brains are not digital computers and human thought cannot be analysed as if it were a computer program. Nevertheless, in some respects and in some circumstances, the products of expressive action (e.g. ritual sequences, mythological texts, poems, musical scores, art forms) show marked pattern similarity to the output of a digital computer, and when we attempt to decode such message-bearing systems we usually find that binary discriminations of the YES/NO type are very prominent. And indeed, as my references to brides and widows suggested, the pattern illustrated in Fig. 5 has more general application.

(b) Colour symbolism

Human beings are adapted to discriminate a wide spectrum of colours, but since colour-blind individuals are not very seriously handicapped and since most of the colours that we can discriminate occur in nature only very infrequently, the precise function of our colour sense is not clear.

We have direct signal responses to light and darkness . . . e.g. the eye adjusts itself to 'see in the dark'. But activities which we think of as appropriate to darkness (e.g. sleeping, love-making (?)) are specified by culture rather than by nature.

It is possible that early childhood experiences may 'imprint' particular emotional attitudes towards particular colours. Milk and semen are white, blood is red, faeces are brown. Blood and faeces both turn black with age. These body products are of personal importance to every individual and they are all elements which appear repeatedly in the symbolic coding of colour discriminations. But there do not seem to be any universals. Certainly it is very common to find that *red* is treated as a sign of *danger*, which may be derived from red = blood. But *red* is also quite often associated with *joy* which might come from red = blood = life. Likewise there are many chains of association by which: white/black = good/bad but sometimes 'black is beautiful'. For example among the Lolo of West China the aristocrats were distinguished from the serfs as 'black boned' versus 'white boned', not the other way round.

Since the colour of the visible body may be quickly changed by costume or by paint and the change is only temporary, colour is a very convenient marker of role reversal and is frequently so used. For example European Christians, and in particular Catholics, use the following formulae:

Ordinary lay people engaged in lay activities – clothing of indiscriminate colour

Priests engaged in lay activities – black robes

Priests engaged in religious rites – white robes

A bride (i.e. a woman entering marriage) – white dress with veil

A widow (i.e. a woman leaving marriage) – black dress with veil

Clearly the messages are 'about' sacredness and purity. The colour discriminations can be mapped as before, in Fig. 6.

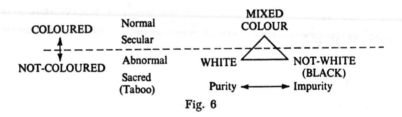

Fig. 6

The same distinctions may turn up in other cultures, even in the same kind of social context, but differently arranged. For example, in traditional China the bride was dressed in bright reds and greens, the widow in unbleached hemp, and an ordinary working-class wife in blue-black (indigo). In the Melanesian Trobriand Islands, as described by Malinowski, the bride wore a grass skirt decorated with bright colours, the widow a grass skirt blackened with soot, and the ordinary working wife a plain unbleached skirt devoid of colour. In each case it is the *set* of contrasts that invites interpretation not the individual colour usage.

Comparably the yellow robe and shaven head of the Buddhist monk is designedly contrasted with the white robe and partly shaven head of the Brahmin priest, and both are contrasted with the ash covered body and long hair of the Indian spirit medium.

Once again the most general point is that symbols occur in sets and that the meaning of particular symbols is to be found in the contrast with other symbols rather than in the symbol as such. But there is the further point that individual symbols have layers of meaning which depend upon what is being contrasted with what. To take the case of the use of unbleached hemp in Chinese first degree mourning. As worn by a widow it contrasts most sharply with the gay colours that are appropriate to a wedding; as worn by a man or a woman at a funeral it is part of an elaborate code which discriminates the relative statuses of a whole range of kinsmen of the deceased (Wolf, 1970).

Because all objects in the visible external world possess attributes of colour, colour difference is always an available means of classification. But an indefinitely large variety of things will fall into any one colour class, so the social metaphors of colour are always potentially polysemic. Even when it is evident that the colour of something has symbolic significance we can never be sure what it is. Each case must be investigated in its particular context.

Victor Turner's extensive analysis of colour symbolism among the Ndembu of Central Africa (Turner, 1967) demonstrate this point in great detail but the following is an example which ties in with what has just been said.

According to the tradition recorded in Buddhist sacred texts the monk's robe is yellow (rather than, say, red or green) so that it shall remind the wearer that the Buddha instructed his followers to pursue a life of such total poverty that they should clothe themselves only in rags taken from corpses. Here the association is 'yellow = death', and there are many other situations in which, in Buddhist Ceylon, the monk is seen as a 'symbol of death'.

But in an important annual ceremony known as *kaṭhina* when the monks are presented with new robes by their parishioners, there is an explicit traditional association between the yellow of the robe and the yellow of the ripening rice harvest. In this case it might appear, at first sight, that 'yellow = life', and *kathina* is certainly a joyful rather than a mournful celebration. This interpretation seems to be reinforced when we learn that the verbal category *dhātu* means both seed grain and semen, as with the Latin term *semen* itself.

Yet this latter association is in turn ambiguous because a third meaning of the term *dhātu* is 'the relic bones of a dead monk', so we are led back again to the Buddhist theological view of life/death as an alternation and the doctrine of the transmigration of souls with the analogy that future redemption springs from buried relics just as future harvests spring from buried seed.

We have here gone a long way beyond colour symbolism but the

59

point about alternative polysemic referents exemplifies a general principle. In social, and especially religious, contexts, it is practically never the case that the communication dyad (*A* stands for *B*) can be directly and uniquely interpreted. *A* starts out as an inchoate metaphysical idea in the mind (p. 37); it acquires manifest physical form by the representational process described in Section 8. But at that stage the manifest form is invariably linked by metonomy and metaphor with a whole string of subsidiary references, which may (or may not) have relevance for the overall social or theological 'meaning'.

(c) *Cooking*

Human beings, like other animals, can subsist on raw food and in part they do. But they also cook their food and moreover they cook and serve it in a great variety of ways. With great insight Lévi-Strauss has observed that these behaviours are expressive as well as technical. He suggests firstly that we cook our food to demonstrate that we are civilised men and not wild animals, and then that we discriminate types of cooking and food preparation as markers of social occasions in accordance with a systematic binary code. Lévi-Strauss's 'culinary triangle' is of the same general type as that of Fig. 5 though much more complex. For details the reader should consult Lévi-Strauss's own account which has appeared in several places (Lévi-Strauss, 1966 (b)) or my own précis (Leach, 1970). In practice the coding is probably less standardised than Lévi-Strauss originally seemed to suggest, but there is certainly 'something in it'. We *do* use the consumption of different kinds of food and drink, specially prepared and served, as prototype markers of particular social occasions, and the way this is done within any single cultural context is certainly patterned in a systematic way.

Almost any kind of ceremonial anywhere involves eating and/or drinking at some point in the proceedings and the kind of food and drink involved is never random. Live food animals, dead food animals, prepared uncooked food, prepared cooked food, are major components in almost every system of ritually circumscribed gift exchange. Special foods such as 'wedding cakes' or 'roast turkey and cranberry sauce' have special easily recognised associations with particular occasions.

All this is quite plain from any careful study of any detailed ethnographic text. Lévi-Strauss's contribution has been to suggest that such binary oppositions as raw/cooked, cooked/rotten, roast/boiled, boiled/smoked constitute distinctive features in a code, and that they are used as such in ritual performance and in mythology. It remains a moot point whether this is always so, but Lévi-Strauss has demonstrated

60

convincingly that it is certainly sometimes so. This is one way in which we *can* give material expression to inchoate ideas in the mind, and once that is appreciated the patterning of food behaviour in all its aspects takes on a new kind of interest.

(d) *Bodily mutilations*

Changes of social status are very frequently indicated by bodily mutilation. The most common are circumcision of males, clitoridechtomy of females, shaving of the head, removal of teeth, scarification, tattooing, ear boring.

At one level such customs have the same implication as a change of costume; a new visible external appearance is a mark of a new social status. Of those listed, shaving the head has the special feature that it is reversible; the hair will grow again after it has been shorn, so it is specially appropriate as a metaphor for the reversal of social time that is called for in rites of transition (Section 7). For example, a widow may shave her head on entering the state of mourning and let it grow again when she returns to normal life. In contrast, irreversible mutilations are more likely to mark permanent stages in social maturation, e.g. the uncircumcised male is a social infant, the circumcised male is a social adult.

Most mutilations involve the removal of a part of the body boundary – foreskin, clitoris, hair, teeth . . . and the rite of removal is very commonly seen as one of purification. The logic of the situation here is related to what was said earlier (Section 7) about the ambiguity of boundaries and their association with taboo.

Mary Douglas has summarised the argument neatly in her aphorism 'Dirt is matter out of place.' Earth in the garden is just earth; it is normal matter in its normal place. Earth in the kitchen is *dirt*; it is matter out of place. The more sharply we define our boundaries, the more conscious we become of the dirt that has ambiguously got onto the wrong side of the frontier. Boundaries become dirty by definition and we devote a great deal of effort to keeping them clean, just so that we can preserve confidence in our category system.

Archaeology and comparative ethnography alike show very clearly that, throughout history and throughout the world, human societies of all kinds have attached enormous ritual importance to thresholds and gateways. The military aspects of the matter are very marginal; the elaboration of points of entry is social-psychological. Individuals move in and out across the threshold, but it is essential for our *moral* security that this should not lead to confusion about the difference between the inside and the outside. There must be a physical discontinuity, clean and portentous.

61

But the principles that apply here to territorial space apply equally to social space and social time.

When we draw a social distinction between an infant and an adult the boundary is artificial; there is no biological point of discontinuity so we must make one. The act of violence, the physical mutilation of the body, marks a break point, a threshold, a point of entry. It then becomes logical to declare that whatever has been thus removed from the body is 'matter out of place', it is dirt. By its removal the purity of our social categories has been preserved, the mutilated body has been cleansed.

The opposition clean/dirty has deep psychological roots. Every individual child, as it develops a consciousness of identity, necessarily becomes concerned with the question 'What am I?', 'Where is the boundary of myself?' The exuviae of the human body present particular difficulty. 'Are my faeces, my urine, my semen, my sweat, a part of me or not a part of me?' By analogy with what I have just said, the orifices of the human body constitute gateways and all exuviae are 'matter out of place', like the by-products of ritual mutilation. They should logically therefore become a focus of taboo. And indeed they do. In most societies, as in our own, body products such as I have listed are the prototype of 'dirt'.

But there is a built-in paradox in such formulations. Individuals do not live in society as isolated individuals with clear-cut boundaries; they exist as individuals interconnected in a network by relations of power and domination. Power, in this sense, resides in the interfaces between individuals, in ambiguous boundaries. The logical paradox is that (i) I can only be completely sure of what I am if I cleanse myself of all boundary dirt, but (ii) a completely clean 'I' with no boundary dirt would have no interface relations with the outside world or with other individuals. Such an 'I' would be free from the domination of others but would in turn be wholly impotent. The inference is the opposition:

$$\text{clean/dirty} = \text{impotence/potency}$$

and hence that *power is located in dirt*.

This paradox is responsible for a vast variety of religious practice, and for the tendency, which we encounter everywhere, for holiness to be attributed *both* to ascetic *and* to ecstatic behaviour. This distinction is considered further in Section 16.

(e) *Noise and silence*

The foregoing discussion of the dirtiness and potency of bodily exuviae has implications for our understanding of the ritual value of noise. Preverbal infantile noises – crying, babbling and, above all, farting – are a kind of exuviae; they come from within the body and end up outside it. They are a marked focus of taboo.

Noises of this sort are a part of Nature and they serve to mark the boundary between 'me' and the world outside. It seems significant therefore that Culture has repeatedly come to use artificial noise for just the same kind of boundary marking purpose. Drum beating, horn blowing, cymbal clashing, the firing off of guns and fire-crackers, the ringing of bells, organised cheering and so on are regularly used as markers of temporal and spatial boundaries, but the boundaries are metaphysical as well as physical.

Bugle calls and bell ringing mark the time of day; fanfares of trumpets mark the entrance of important persons; gunshots and fire-crackers are characteristic markers of funeral processions and weddings; the end of time is to be signalled by The Last Trump; thunder is the voice of God. So:

$$\text{noise/silence} = \text{sacred/profane.}$$

General formulae of this sort pose problems about human universals. Are there some surface features of culture which occur everywhere? I suspect that the answer to that question is 'No'. Even though some structured relationships among cultural elements are very common there are always likely to be special cases where values get reversed. For example Bauman (1974) has pointed out that it is a fundamental tenet of Quaker theology that God communicates directly with each devout individual who is prepared to sit in silence and await divine inspiration. Here then, in the Quaker case:

$$\text{silence/noise} = \text{sacred/profane.}$$

The point that I have just made is one that applies to all the examples of binary coding which have been mentioned in this section. Any 'bit' of cultural information which is conveyed by the binary contrast X/Y (e.g. white/black) could just as easily be conveyed by the binary contrast Y/X (black/white), and since all metaphoric associations are in the last analysis arbitrary, it is always likely that any particular significant contrast which occurs in one ethnographic context will turn up in reversed form in some other.

Such reversals may themselves be significant. Local custom is quite often organised not simply on the basis that 'we, the X people, do things differently from them, the Y people' but on the principle 'our X customs are correct; those lousy Y people just across the valley are obvious barbarians, they do everything back to front!'

The question of whether a particular tribal community burn or bury their dead, or whether their houses are round or rectangular may sometimes have no functional explanation other than that the people concerned want to show themselves different from and superior to their neighbours down the road. In turn their neighbours, whose customs

63

are just the opposite, feel equally confident that their way of doing things is correct and superior. The more similar the general cultural patterning of the two communities, the more critical will be the significance which is attached to such minor points of reversal. English-speaking Americans and Englishmen should be able to think of dozens of relevant examples. What you should do with your knife and fork after you have finished eating not only differs according to whether you are in England, France or the United States, it is 'bad manners' if you get it wrong!

14. *Mating prescriptions and proscriptions*

Newcomers to the subject are often puzzled and bored by the enormous amount of space which the authors of social anthropological monographs devote to the detailed description and analysis of kinship terminologies and marriage rules. Most of the authors concerned would be hard put to it to justify what they do, but certainly the anthropological study of kinship, in this style, bears very directly on the theme of this essay.

In the first place both kinship terms and formal marriage rules constitute distinguishable 'sets' of metonymically related cultural items – like the individual items of clothing which go to make up a particular costume. Furthermore, as we move across the ethnographic map, we often find that neighbouring communities of broadly similar culture adopt strikingly different conventions regarding the classification of kin. A semiotic structuralist style of analysis of the kind I have been describing suggests that in circumstances of this sort the overall pattern should be viewed as one of successive transformation rather than simple difference. Lévi-Strauss's celebrated *The Elementary Structures of Kinship* (1949) was an attempt to apply this notion of transformation to a whole range of kinship systems stretching geographically from Australia to Northern Siberia! It was not altogether successful but the underlying idea remains important.

Secondly the concepts involved in kinship terms and marriage rules provide particularly tricky examples of the kinds of problem which were raised in Section 3. Notions such as 'marriage' and 'fatherhood' are, in the first instance, 'ideas' generated in the mind; they are not descriptive of any material objective 'thing' in the world out-there. Consequently the discussion of kinship categories and marriage rules is very easily converted into a kind of algebra. It is presumably for this reason that it has always proved particularly congenial to those whose approach to anthropological evidence is rational rather than empirical (see Section 1).

On the other hand, because all human societies distinguish categories of kin and recognise mating conventions which are analogous, at least up to a point, to the institution which the English language

65

describes as 'marriage', it is easy to persuade oneself that rationalist discussions of kinship algebra relate quite directly to the observable empirical facts of kinship in contrasted ethnographic situations, and this suggests that Lévi-Strauss was right in thinking that structuralist ideas had immediate application to the study of kinship.

My advice is that you tackle this whole branch of anthropological enquiry with great caution. There is certainly a sense in which the study of kinship and marriage on a comparative basis is absolutely central to the theory and practice of social anthropology, but the difficulties should not be underestimated. The connection between the observable facts on the ground and the formal kinship algebra which appears in anthropological monographs is often very indirect. Moreover any form of analysis which has the effect of separating off kinship as a thing-in-itself, which can sensibly be discussed in isolation from the cultural matrix in which it is embedded, will prove thoroughly misleading.

As a matter of fact my own view is that the ethnography of kinship can *only* be understood if the facts are analysed by some kind of structuralist technique, but, as far as kinship is concerned, you will need to have a pretty thorough grasp of the methodology before you can get much value out of its application.

In an 'introduction' such as this the variety of marriage rules is easier to discuss than the variety of systems of kinship classification. The variety is very striking. Some societies deem it a cardinal sin for a man to mate with any woman who is not a recognised relative of some sort; others with equal vigour prohibit all matings between recognised relatives. Some consider marriage with a first cousin particularly desirable, others particularly undesirable. There are rules which have the implication that the only proper mate for a man is his mother's mother's brother's daughter's daughter; at the other extreme there are societies which permit mating with almost any woman other than a mother or a full sister. Anthropologists have argued at great length and with great heat about the general and particular significance of such rules without arriving at any consensus.

Some parts of the 'logic' appear self-evident.
(i) Any rule which has the implication (for a man) that 'women of category A are marriageable but women of category B are not' is part of a system of social classification which serves to map out the social environment of the individual concerned.
(ii) Any rule which has the implication (for a man) that 'if the category of marriageable women includes the sister of X, then my own sister falls into the category of marriageable women for X' also implies that I and X are, in some fundamental sense, of *equal* standing. The basic principle of reciprocity applies (see p. 6).

66

The rule says that I and X are expected to exchange things of like kind. If I marry your sister, you will marry mine. This puts us precisely on a par.

(iii) Correspondingly any rule which has the contrary implication (for a man) that 'if the category of marriageable women includes the sister of X, then my own sister does *not* fall into the category of marriageable women for X' also implies that 'I' and X are in some fundamental sense, of *unequal* standing. The rule says that if I marry your sister, you cannot marry mine; in some way we are not on a par.

Even these apparently self-evident formal algebraic principles need qualification in the light of the empirical evidence, but it certainly is the case that rules which specify the categories of males and females who may or may not mate with one another are of very great importance for the empirical structuring of all self-perpetuating human social systems. Furthermore, our ideas about how society is ordered, or ought to be ordered, are very often expressed in attitudes towards particular types of marriage possibility. You only have to consider the strength and variety of explicit and implicit rules which serve to inhibit marriages across frontiers of 'class' and 'race' and 'caste' to see the importance of such modes of classification. But beyond that I am hardly prepared to go except to make four brief observations.

(I) Exogamy rules which prohibit matings between members of the same social segment of a single overall system – e.g. as in a great variety of segmentary unilineal descent systems in many parts of the world – not only have the effect of reinforcing the other criteria by which the segments are defined, but also have the negative implication of knitting the whole system together. Since we cannot make marriage alliances with members of our own group we need to make alliances with others. You need to bear in mind however that, in such cases, the rules of exogamy are concerned with *marriage*. The rules governing actual sexual behaviour, i.e. rules about 'incest', are usually far less clear-cut and are best considered quite separately from rules about marriage.

(II) Endogamy rules which prohibit matings between members of different social segments of the same overall system – e.g. an Indian high caste girl with a low caste man, a South African white with a South African black, a Jew with a non-Jew – invariably generate an enormous amount of emotional heat. This exemplifies the point made in Section 13(d) about the taboo which attaches to boundaries *per se*. In cases of this sort however the rules are concerned with sexual relationships as such as well as with marriage, and it is breach of the *sexual* taboo that arouses emotion.

(III) Religious sects (Jews, Quakers, Catholics) very often make it a test of orthodoxy that a man and his wife must both be members of the faith; the rule here is both expressive and functional, it 'says' 'we are of the same faith', it also ensures that the solidarity of the faith is likely to be perpetuated into later generations.

If sectarian groups of this kind were successful in operating their rule of strict endogamy over a period of centuries, the sect would in the end become racially distinct. This simple statement of fact, applied to the Jews, shows how important it is for the social anthropologist to be aware of the distinction between ethnographic facts and normative ideas.

It has been a constantly reiterated tenet of the Jewish religion, for at least 2500 years, that Jews should only mate with other Jews. Had they kept this rule, the Jews would indeed now be a race apart. But in fact the genetic evidence makes it quite clear that there is no part of the world in which the racial characteristics of the Jews are significantly different from those of their neighbours. It therefore follows that the Jews as a group have not maintained their rules of endogamy.

In the circumstances it is highly paradoxical that, over the centuries, the persecution of Jewish communities by their Christian neighbours has consistently been based on racial rather than religious prejudice!

The general point is that all rules about marriage and mating are much more concerned with ideas than with facts on the ground. They are assertions about what ought to be the case. What actually happens is usually something very different.

(IV) And finally there is the point that rules of type (iii) above quite frequently take the form: 'I (a male) may marry my mother's brother's daughter but my sister may not marry her mother's brother's son.' When this form of rule occurs in the context of a system of unilineal descent groups it has the implication that localised unilineal descent groups are paired as 'wife givers' and 'wife receivers' and the relationship 'wife giver'/'wife receiver' is indicated as being one of inequality. This inequality is often built into the structure of the local political ideology. The literature on this topic is extensive, see, e.g. Leach (1954).

15. *Logic and mytho-logic*

I want now to return to the problem which I raised earlier (Section 6) of how far we can distinguish the logic of technical actions from the pseudo-logic of expressive actions.

In our own Western, literate, mechanically organised society, so much 'true' Aristotelian logic is built into the cultural system that we mostly take it for granted that logic of this kind is an essential component of common sense. Yet in practice we only exploit formal logical principles in the relatively rare instances in which we are seeking to convey exact information at a distance using a single channel of communication, as in writing a letter or a book or speaking to someone over the telephone. When two people are in fact to face communication, so that they can use several channels of sensory information simultaneously – touch, sight, hearing and so on – the logical ordering of individual messages is much less obvious.

If you record unrehearsed conversation on tape you will find that on play-back very little of it is immediately comprehensible; yet, in context, all those present would have understood what was being said. This is because, in its original setting, the spoken utterance was only part of a larger whole. It had a metonymic (sign) relationship with everything else that was going on in the room at the same time, and this non-verbal 'other' was also conveying part of the message.

But the same argument applies the other way round. When an anthropologist tries to decode a set of non-verbal indices he needs to remember that he has only got part of the evidence. The signs and symbols he is investigating are loosely hitched together like the words and half-finished sentences of a casual conversation rather than as the carefully constructed, self-sufficient, paragraphs of a book.

But the pseudo-logic (mytho-logic) of expressive behaviour has other peculiarities. These are specially easy to recognise if we consider the case of religious discourse.

When we are engaged in an ordinary technical action we take it for granted that if an entity A is distinguished from an entity B, it cannot simultaneously be held that A and B are identical. In theological argument just the opposite is the case.

69

Christianity affords some very striking examples: the concept of the Virgin-Mother of God is one; the proposition that God the Son was 'begotten' of God the Father, even though God the Father, God the Son, and God the Holy Ghost have been one and the same and identical from the beginning, is another. Admittedly even devout Christians have great difficulty in 'understanding' such mysteries, but it certainly cannot be argued that just because religious propositions are non-logical (in the ordinary sense) they must be meaningless.

Religious statements certainly have meaning, but it is a meaning which refers to a metaphysical reality, whereas ordinary logical statements have a meaning which refers to physical reality. The non-logicality of religious statements is itself 'part of the code', it is an index of what such statements are about, it tells us that we are concerned with metaphysical rather than physical reality, with belief rather than knowledge.

This distinction is important. In normal English usage we do *not* say 'I believe that $3 \times 3 = 9$'. We treat the arithmetic formula as a simple logical statement of fact. We *know* it to be true. On the other hand, whenever we make religious statements, we invoke the concept of belief. 'I *believe* in God the Father . . .' The use of the formula 'I believe in . . .' amounts to a warning; it is equivalent to: 'In what follows the rules of ordinary logic do not apply.'

One characteristic feature of such non-logic (mytho-logic) is that metaphor is treated as metonymy. For example, consider the following statements: (1) God is a father, (2) God is a son, (3) God is a Holy Spirit. If these three assertions are regarded as separate metaphors then the words 'father', 'son', 'Holy Spirit' are, in my terminology, alternative *symbols* for a single metaphysical concept 'in the mind'. But the peculiarity of religious discourse is that it denies that such formulae are metaphoric; they are said to be 'true' and simultaneously 'true'. At that level, the three key words are brought into metonymic relationship, they become mutually interdependent *signs*. But then the terms father/son form a couple and we introduce the 'non-sense' whereby God is both father and son to himself. Even so there is sense behind the non-sense.

Mytho-logical statements conflict with the logical rules of ordinary physical experience but they can make sense 'in the mind' so long as the speaker and his listener, or the actor and his audience, share the same conventional ideas about the attributes of metaphysical time and space and of metaphysical objects. These attributes have a certain general uniformity throughout human society, and in the next section I shall consider some such universals.

70

16. *Basic cosmology*

At the heart of the matter is our recognition that man is mortal and that illness threatens death. The central doctrine of all religion is the denial that death implies the automatic annihilation of the individual self.

But if 'I' am to survive after death as some sort of 'other being', then this 'other being' must be located in some 'other world' in some 'other time'. The most fundamental characteristic of such 'otherness' is that it is the reverse of ordinary experience.

Concepts of deity derive from a similar reversal. As human beings we are conscious of our impotence; we are only able to modify the conditions of our material existence in very slight degree. But any concept of impotence implies the notion of omnipotence, which is again 'other'. Deity, an omnipotent 'other being' occupying an 'other world' in 'other time', thus has very similar attributes to the deceased 'other self', and, in eschatological theorising, the two kinds of 'other world' are often merged, so that deceased ancestors become gods.

But this poses a mytho-logical puzzle. If Deity, the source of 'power', is located in the other world, how can human beings have access to that power?

Religious practice is a response to this question. It is concerned with establishing a mediating bridge between 'this world' and 'the other' through which the omnipotent power of deity may be channelled to bring aid to impotent men.

Here let me remind you of what has been said previously about the innate sacred-taboo quality of all boundaries, which derives from their ambiguity and about the closely related principle that 'power is located in dirt' (pp. 35, 62).

The mediating bridge is represented, in a material sense, by 'holy places' which are both in this world, and not in this world – e.g. churches which are said to be 'the House of God'. Control over the mediating bridge is exercised by 'holy men' (priests, hermits, shamans, mediums, inspired prophets) who are credited with the capability of establishing communication with other world powers even while they are still alive in this world. In mythology, as distinct from cult practice,

71

the mediating bridge can also be occupied by incarnate deities, who manage, by an elision of metaphor and metonymy, to be both human beings and gods at the same time.

One other generalisation is possible. Because sexual intercourse can be seen to be life-generating, and because eschatological theory is concerned with the denial of death, the equation which we make in English between potency as power and potency as sexuality is extremely common. The 'power of the Holy Spirit' is magical power in a very general sense, but it is also the capacity to make women pregnant.

The topographical details of such metaphysical cosmology may vary greatly. The 'other world' may be above the sky, below the sea, in the mountains, in the forest, across the bay, across the desert. The only thing that can be said about it in general is that it is *not* here and now! Frequently it is differentiated into layers and contrasts – e.g. Heaven, Hell, Purgatory. But to some extent at least the opposition 'This world (of physical knowledge)' versus 'The other world (of metaphysical belief)' nearly always becomes confused with such oppositions as 'Human/Animal', 'Tame/Wlid', 'Culture/Nature', where Culture may be defined as 'the way of life which *we* humans experience in *our* society' (i.e. 'Civilisation') and Nature is everything else.

The mediator, whether he is a 'real' human being (e.g. a shaman) or a mythological god–man then takes on liminal attributes – he is *both* mortal *and* immortal, human *and* animal, tame *and* wild.

For example, Biblical prophets, who are emissaries between the City of God and the Cities of Men, reside in between 'in the wilderness'. Gaṇeśa, the Hindu deity who is particularly associated with thresholds and is the doorkeeper of holy places, has a human body and an elephant head. In totemic systems the totemic ancestors are *both* categories of things *and* species 'in Nature' *and* categories of groups 'in human society'.

This kind of elision of opposites is, as I have already emphasised, 'nonsense' in terms of normal logic but is fully consistent with mytho-logic.

Consider the following syllogism:

(1) Since deities are immortal it is anomalous that a god/goddess should reproduce himself/herself by sexual intercourse.

(2) Since men are mortal it is anomalous that a man/woman should not reproduce himself/herself by sexual intercourse.

(3) It is therefore anomalous for a god–man either to reproduce himself by sexual intercourse or not to do so.

A vast amount of religious belief and practice in a great variety of quite different cultural systems can be 'explained' by this paradox. At the level of myth it is responsible for the kind of contradiction that I have mentioned already – the Son of God *is* God the Father, Aiyanar *is* Śiva, Horus *is* Osiris. At the level of practice it produces uncertainty as to whether overindulgence or underindulgence in sexual activity is the true mode of holy otherness.

The potency of deities is closely entangled with the potency of sex. The great gods of classical and oriental mythology were notably licentious. And clearly any mythological being who is classed as an ancestor must be credited with some degree of sexual indulgence. Yet it is very common to find that men who aspire to extreme holiness adopt a regime of sexual asceticism. Sometimes they explain their behaviour in terms of a theory that loss of semen in sexual intercourse implies loss of 'power', sometimes in terms of a belief that abstention from sex makes a man (or woman) 'like a god', and sometimes in terms of a simple dogma that sexual activity is evil in itself. Yet divine ancestors are necessarily the patriarchal prototypes of sainthood! Such contradictions are handled in many different ways but in every case the equivocations of mytho-logic have the effect of masking their inconsistencies. Here are some examples:

One solution to the difficulty is to have the first ancestor produce children only in extreme old age. Adam begets Seth at the age of 130; Abraham begets Isaac at the age of 100. Likewise sex and sin are separated by having the predestined prophet saint born to a saintly woman who is either long past the (natural) age of childbearing or otherwise barren, like Sarah, Rebekah, Rachel, Elizabeth, etc.

But this does not get over the third leg of my syllogism. If the male ancestor is 'really' divine and immortal, sexuality and procreation is an irrelevance; he should not have to concern himself with producing descendants. But if the ancestor is 'really' human, he must be credited with the normal appetites of normal man.

One common mythic solution is to have the god–man cohabit with a harlot, or to have the semi-divine ascetic ancestor seduced by the wiles of an 'evil' woman who then becomes a sainted ancestress. Sex remains a necessary evil, the sexual potency of the saint is recognised, but he retains his saintly asceticism in the face of corruption. A good example is the Biblical story of Tamar's seduction of her father-in-law Judah (Genesis ch. 38). Comparably in the New Testament the humanity of Jesus is affirmed by the repeated assertion that he associates with publicans and sinners, among whom is reckoned Mary Magdalene. But simultaneously Jesus' divinity is affirmed by the assertion that God is the son of Mary the Virgin who is also God's consort. In mythological terms Mary the sinless Virgin and Mary the Sinner are 'the same person'.

This Christian pattern is strikingly similar to that found in Hindu mythology, especially in the story of Śiva and Parvati. Śiva is the most ascetic of all yogis and his divine power derives from asceticism; yet, as

73

the consort of Parvati, the most beautiful woman in the universe, who was expressly created to seduce the unseducable Śiva, he is the most passionate of all lovers.

The ambiguities of the myth, taken as a whole, turn on the fact that the gods have guaranteed both that Parvati shall have a child by Śiva and that she shall not have a child at all. In the end Skanda [Aiyanar] (who is another form of Śiva himself) is rated to be 'the son of Śiva and Parvati', though Parvati has not given birth to any child (see O'Flaherty, 1973).

Stories of this kind are not invented simply as exercises in the art of paradox; they contain practical implication. The devout Brahmin has a moral duty to produce male offspring, but he also has a moral duty to move progressively in the direction of sexual asceticism. The myth provides a charter for both modes of activity.

On the other hand the paradoxical nature of mythological stories is itself a part of their message. What is not natural is supernatural!

These examples of mythological inconsistency illustrate a general principle.

Asceticism is a means to personal purity; ecstacy is a means to mystical power. Typically, the things and behaviours which are deemed dirty in an ascetic cult are regarded as a source of power in an ecstatic cult. The sexual act is the prototype of evil for the one, a symbol of the divine for the others. Both attitudes commonly exist side by side within the same cultural system. The notions of divine purity, achieved through asceticism, and of divine power, achieved through ecstacy, are interdependent concepts, the one implies the other.

Yet religious practice necessarily represents this binary dyad in terms of separable opposites – e.g. shaven head/long hair, castrated eunuch/sexual athlete – and cult behaviour usually stresses one half of the dichotomy at the expense of the other. The metaphysical bridge across the boundary between 'this world' and 'the other world' is *either* under the control of ascetic priests *or* under the control of ecstatic spirit mediums (shamans). When the two get mixed together embarrassment ensues; the mysticism of Saint Teresa with its elaborate sexual metaphors can only be accommodated with the greatest difficulty to the austerely asexual orthodoxy of the Catholic Church which insists on maintaining a celibate priesthood.

Before leaving this topic I would like you to look back at Section 14 and think further about the ambiguities involved in notions of unilineal descent, endogamy and exogamy. The ambiguity is clearest in the case of patrilineal descent associated with lineage exogamy. Every married woman first joins the local lineage group as an alien. She is intrinsically evil; a foreign object, a sexual object, dirty. But in due course she becomes the mother of new members of the lineage. In this second

74

capacity she is intrinsically good, the very criterion of virtue and cleanliness, the antithesis of a sexual object. The moral polarity thus involves the following equivalents

$$\frac{\text{wife}}{\text{mother}} : \frac{\text{sexual}}{\text{asexual}} : \frac{\text{dirty}}{\text{clean}} : \frac{\text{sinful}}{\text{sinless}}$$

The pattern, you will notice, is that of the two Mary's of Christian mythology to which I have already referred.

This observation needs to be considered in the light of anthropological theories concerning the origin of the incest taboo. There are many such theories, none of them satisfactory. One version, which has been advocated in different forms by both Tylor and Lévi-Strauss, is that the core of the incest taboo is the prohibition of sex relations between brother and sister. Rules of exogamy call for the exchange of women between male dominated groups. In order to marry a wife I must be prepared to give away a sister.

The argument of this Section suggests a different possibility, equally structural, but perhaps rather closer to the readily observable facts of human psychology. The suggestion is that it is the irreversibility of the transformation wife → mother, the absolute polar opposition between these two categories, and the ever recurrent need to be on guard against the kind of ambiguity which is reflected in the Hindu and Christian mythologies of Parvati and Mary which lie at the heart of the matter. It is a new version of Malinowski's thesis that the 'function' of the incest taboo is to prevent a confusion of social roles.

But this latter kind of incest theory has its limitations also. A fully adequate theory would need to conform to the principles which I have been stressing throughout this essay. It would need to treat all varieties of sexual offence as forming a set and then examine the permutations of their interrelationships. It would not be just a matter of considering the connection between exogamy and brother–sister incest, or between the status of wife and the status of mother, it would have to consider a whole range of categories of sexual sin and sexual misdemeanour – incest, bestiality, homosexuality, rape, adultery, fornification and so on – and examine how and why they are distinguished and where and why the frontier between legitimate and illegitimate sexual behaviour is drawn where it is, when it is. That study has not yet been made, but when it is made, it will need to take account of many of the structural transformations we have been considering.

17. *Rites of transition (rites de passage)*

I have already remarked that most ritual occasions are concerned with movement across social boundaries from one social status to another, living man to dead ancestor, maiden to wife, sick and contaminated to healthy and clean, etc. The ceremonies concerned have the double function of proclaiming the change of status and of magically bringing it about (see Sections 7 and 11). From another point of view they are the interval markers in the progression of social time.

In a very broad sense all transition rites have a certain three-phase similarity of structure.

The initiate who is undergoing a change of status must first be separated from his (her) initial role. This separation may be represented in a variety of ways all of which may appear as part of the same ritual proceedings, e.g.

(a) the initiate may move in procession from position A to position B
(b) the initiate may take off his (her) original clothing
(c) sacrificial animals may be killed so that the life is separated from the carcase or sacrificial objects may be split in half
(d) surface 'dirt' of the initiate may be removed by ritual washing, shaving, etc.

In general these initial rites of separation have the effect of removing the initiate from normal existence; he (she) becomes temporarily an abnormal person existing in abnormal time.

Following the 'rite of separation' there follows an interval of social timelessness (see p. 34) which, as reckoned by the clock, may have a duration of a few moments or extend for months. Examples of the latter, more prolonged, kind of marginal state are the honeymoon of a bride and the mourning of a widow. The general characteristic of such rites of marginality (*rites de marge*) is that the initiate is kept physically apart from ordinary people, either by being sent away from the normal home surroundings altogether or by being temporarily housed in an enclosed space from which ordinary people are excluded.

The social separation is further emphasised by subjecting the initiate to all kinds of special prescriptions and proscriptions regarding food, clothing, and movement generally.

So far as ordinary people are concerned the initiate is at this state 'contaminated with holiness'; being in a sacred state, he (she) is also dangerous and therefore 'dirty'. Consistent with this ideology, the rituals which bring the initiate back into normal life again nearly always include procedures, such as ritual washing, designed to remove the contamination.

Finally, in the third phase, the initiate is brought back into normal society and aggregated to his (her) new role. The actual proceedings in a rite of aggregation are often very similar to those of the initial rite of separation but in reverse, i.e. processions move in the reverse direction from B to A, the special costume worn during the 'marginal state' is removed and a new normal costume appropriate to the new normal social status is put on, sacrifices are repeated, food restrictions removed, shaven heads grow their hair again, etc.

But role reversal may be expressed in a variety of ways e.g. by such contrasts as fasting/feasting; exaggerated formality in which every individual is in a 'correct' explicit uniform/exaggerated informality in which costumes are dishevelled and transvestism is prominent; reversing a sequence of events. The 'logic' of what is happening is seldom obvious.

The general three-phase scheme outlined above is illustrated by Fig. 7. The extent to which any particular sequence of ritual activity

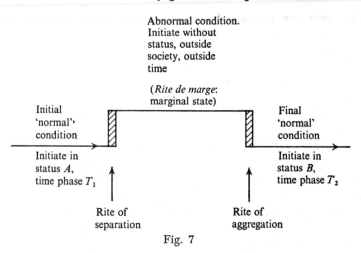

Fig. 7

can be seen to fit will depend to some extent upon the ingenuity and imagination of the anthropologist who is making the analysis, but I personally find such diagrams helpful.

In this context one further generalisation has fairly widespread application.

Since every discontinuity in social time is the end of one period and the beginning of another, and since birth/death is a self-evident 'natural' representation of beginning/end, death and rebirth symbolism is appropriate to all rites of transition and is palpably manifest in a wide variety of cases.

In the case of mortuary ritual it is often a matter of dogma that death is only a gateway to future life. Conversely the rituals of circumcision, head shaving, knocking out teeth, and other bodily mutilations which so commonly mark the initiate's first entry into adult society, are metaphors not only of purification (see p. 62) but also of death. The child must die before the adult can be born.

In some cases mythology makes this quite explicit. In Genesis (chs. 17, 21, 22) the Jewish rite of circumcision is a 'token' of Abraham's acceptance of the covenant by which, provided Abraham shows his obedience to God, God guarantees Abraham countless descendants. But before Isaac can fulfil his role of becoming the founder ancestor of the Israelite nation, he must first be circumcised and then 'almost' be sacrificed by his father.

18. *The logic of sacrifice*

The argument of the last two sections has again become very abstract and you may well be asking yourself how such very general theory can have practical use. How could it help the anthropologist to understand what is going on when he or she encounters a totally unfamiliar chunk of culturally defined behaviour?

The present section applies the theory to the procedures of sacrifice. This seems an appropriate test case because, although animal sacrifice is a very common feature of religious ritual, most of my readers will have had no first-hand acquaintance with such performances. If we now examine the details of a description of a sacrifice, how far does the theory in fact help to elucidate what is going on?

The central puzzle about sacrifice centres around the metaphor of death. What has the killing of animals got to do with communication between Man and Deity or with changing the social status of individuals? My own immediate problem is of a different kind. How can I describe enough of the total context of a typical sacrificial rite for you to get some feeling of the complexity of the problems which face the anthropological analyst when he meets with such performances in the field? For you must understand that in any fieldwork situation many things are going on at once. At the very least, any ritual activity has visual, verbal, spatial and temporal dimensions; in addition, noise, smell, taste, touch may all be relevant. Many action sequences will probably be repeated several times over but often with slight variations at each repetition. How then should the observer discriminate between the significant, the accidental and the redundant?

First let me review the theory as such. The argument of Sections 7, 11 and 17 suggests two rather different models of how religious ritual serves to express a relationship between the world of physical experience and the other world of metaphysical imagination.

Model I was schematised in Fig. 4 (p. 35) which I reproduce, with different wording, as Fig. 8. The concept of the Other World is generated by direct inversion of the characteristics of ordinary experience. This World is inhabited by mortal, impotent, men, who live out their lives in normal time in which events happen in sequence, one after another. In this world we get older and older 'all the time' and in the end we die. The Other World is inhabited by immortal, omnipotent gods, who exist perpetually in abnormal time in which past, present and future all coexist 'simultaneously'.

In this first model 'power', conceived as the source of health, life, fertility, political influence, wealth . . . is located in the other world and the purpose of religious performance is to provide a bridge, or channel of communication, through which the power of the gods may be made available to otherwise impotent men.

This World and the Other World are here conceived as separate topographical spaces separated by a liminal zone which partakes of the qualities of both. It is the liminal zone which is the focus of ritual activity (e.g. churches, graveyards, shrines). The metaphysical 'per-

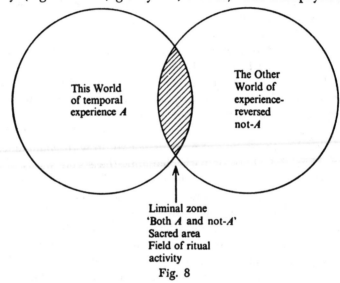

This World
of temporal
experience *A*

The Other
World of
experience-
reversed
not-*A*

Liminal zone
'Both *A* and not-*A*'
Sacred area
Field of ritual
activity
Fig. 8

sons' to whom the ritual activity is addressed are associated with these sacred places and are typically regarded as ancestors, saints, or in-carnate deities – beings who were formerly ordinary men who died ordinary deaths but who have now become immortal gods. Like the liminal zone itself they partake of qualities drawn both from This World and the Other World.

The human beings who perform the ritual activities are likewise abnormal by the criteria applied to ordinary mortal men. They may be *priests*, who are required to put themselves into a special condition of 'ritual purity' before they can undertake the main ritual, or they may be *shamans*, spirit mediums who have acquired an abnormal capacity to put themselves into trances, in which state they are supposed to communicate directly with beings from the Other World.

82

The alternative *Model II* is represented by Fig. 7 (p. 78). The emphasis here is on metaphysical time rather than metaphysical space or semi-metaphysical persons. Social time is made to appear discontinuous by inserting intervals of liminal, sacred non-time into the continuous flow of normal secular time.

According to this second model the purpose of ritual activity, which need not necessarily have an explicitly religious form, is to bring about a transition from normal to abnormal time at the beginning of the ceremony and another transition from abnormal to normal time at the end of it (as in Section 17).

The two models are complementary rather than contradictory and either or both may in practical situations throw light on the structure of observed ritual performances and the purposes that lie behind them.

So how about animal sacrifice?

One view, which quite often appears to be supported by the language in which people describe their own sacrifices is that a sacrificial offering is a gift, or tribute, or fine paid to the gods. The performance is an expression of the principle of reciprocity. By making a gift to the gods, the gods are compelled to give back benefits to man.

Model I suggests that part of the logic by which men should come to suppose that killing an animal constitutes a gift to the gods depends upon the following metaphorical associations. The souls of dead men pass from the normality of This World to the abnormality of the liminal zone and then, by further transformation, become immortal ancestor deities in the Other World. If we want to make a gift to a being in the Other World, the 'soul', that is to say the metaphysical essence, of the gift must be transmitted along the same route as is travelled by the soul of a dead man. We must therefore first kill the gift so that its metaphysical essence is separated from its material body, and then transfer the essence to the Other World by rituals which are analogous to those of a funeral.

At one level this does seem to be how people think about their sacrifices though the metaphor of gift giving can easily prove misleading. Gods do not need presents from men; they require signs of submission. The material body of the sacrificial victim may well be a serious economic cost to the giver of the sacrifice, but, at the metaphysical level, economics is not the issue. What matters is the act of sacrifice as such, which is indeed a symbol of gift giving, but gift giving as an expression of reciprocal relationship (p. 6) rather than material exchange.

In point of fact, as a rule, most of the meat of the slaughtered animal is eaten by members of the 'congregation', who are friends and relatives of the giver of the sacrifice. When this is not the case the animal is likely to be small, or to be replaced by something else of trivial economic value, e.g. there are circumstances when the Nuer (as described by Evans-Pritchard) will replace an ox by a wild cucumber!

In any event, the animal or object sacrificed is a metonymic sign for the donor of the sacrifice. By arranging for a liminal priest to perform the sacrifice in the liminal zone, the donor provides a bridge between the world of the gods and the world of men across which the potency of the gods can flow (toward himself).

Model II suggests a slightly different set of metaphors. As before and as in all rites of transition the paradigm is provided by mortuary ritual. At death a living man becomes, by a process of 'natural' *separation*, a dead corpse plus a ghost-soul. This separation is treated as a 'purification' of the ghost-soul, which is initially deemed to be in limbo, separated from, but still close to, its original domestic environment. But whereas the soul has been purified, that from which it has been separated – i.e. the corpse and the close kin of the deceased – has become polluted.

After an interval, further rituals aggregate the ghost into the category of ancestors and bring back the polluted mourners into normal society by removing their pollution. The general utility of this model is shown by the frequency with which the metaphor of death and rebirth crops up in all sorts of initiations (p. 79).

The paradigmatic idea is that the procedures of the rite *separate* the 'initiate' into two parts – one pure, the other impure. The impure part can then be left behind, while the pure part can be aggregated to the initiate's new status. In the case of sacrifice the sacrificial victim plays the part of the initiate, but since the victim has first been identified with the donor of the sacrifice, the donor is, by vicarious association, likewise purified and initiated into a new ritual status.

From this point of view the sacrifice is a magical act which moves the whole proceedings on to the next stage. The aura of sacredness which surrounds the act of killing ties in with the fact that sacrifices are markers of boundaries in social time (cf. Sections 7, 13(d)).

I propose now to apply this general theory to a specific piece of purported ethnographic description which is readily available to everyone.

The Biblical story of the consecration of Aaron as high priest, which appears in two very similar versions in Exodus and Leviticus, provides a detailed account of sacrificial procedures of a kind that can still be observed at first hand in all sorts of different ethnographic contexts throughout the world. It explicitly brings sacrifice into association with a rite of transition and it also gives special emphasis to the use of sacrifice as a means to the attainment of ritual purification through separation from impurity.

In these Biblical stories the ethnographic context is mythological:

the Israelitish Tabernacle, as described in the text, is culturally, architecturally and archaeologically an impossibility. But the very precise details of the associated rituals are certainly not imaginary. The myth served as a justification for Jewish sacrificial practices associated with the temple at Jerusalem around the third century B.C. At the point in history when the stories were first committed to writing the various categories of behaviour which are distinguished must have corresponded to ethnographic facts which were known to the author at first hand. The similarity to sacrificial procedures which I have myself witnessed in various parts of South East Asia is indeed quite remarkable.

So my suggestion is that you treat these texts 'as if' they represented the notebook record of a contemporary ethnographer. Get hold of a copy of the Bible and, in reading my analysis, check back constantly to the original text as you might well want to do if I were referring to a modern anthropological monograph. Where sacrificial procedure is concerned my main references are to Leviticus chapters 1–10 and 16. Part of this text is very similar to Exodus chapter 29. Various details in Exodus chapters 28 and 30 are also relevant.

The meticulously detailed description of the construction of the Ark and the Tabernacle in Exodus chapters 25–27 needs to be viewed rather differently. It is a model for the layout of a setting for sacrificial procedure, a representation of cosmological space as shown in Fig. 9. This point calls for elaboration.

First of all you have to remember that every religious ritual, no matter whether it takes place at a wayside shrine temporarily erected for the purpose or in a permanent setting such as the sanctuary of a cathedral, is performed within the confines of a stage, the boundaries and segments of which are artificial. At a structural level the components of such stages are highly standardised. There are three essential elements:

Zone 1. The shrine proper, which, in the context of the ritual, becomes extremely sacred. It usually contains some iconic symbol which makes it immediately apparent that this is where the deity is, e.g. an image, an empty seat, a crucifix . . . In the context of the ritual this 'shrine proper' is treated as if it were actually part of the Other World.

Zone 2. The place of assembly of the congregation. The essential point here is that this area must be close to but separated from the shrine proper. In the context of the ritual, ordinary members of the congregation must not enter the shrine proper which is reserved for priests and other religious functionaries.

Zone 3. An area of middle ground on which most of the action of the ritual takes place which is likewise reserved for the priests.

For example, in the context of an uncomplicated form of the Christian communion service, the 'Shrine proper' is the Altar, the 'place of assembly of the congregation' is the whole of the church to the west of the altar rails, 'the middle ground' is the area between the altar and the altar rails. In terms of Fig. 8 (p. 82), Zone 1 corresponds to the right-hand circle, Zone 2 to the left-hand circle, Zone 3 to the liminal area common to both.

Every particular case however will be a variation on this basic theme and, in the Biblical stories, the model by which the empirical setting of the ritual is transformed into cosmological space is somewhat more complicated. It is these additional complications that I have tried to indicate in Fig. 9.

Cosmological space categories	Text categories	
Wild Nature	Outside the camp	
Tame Culture	Inside the camp	
Intermediate Zone *A* Relatively secular	Court of Tabernacle	Place of assembly
Threshold between This World and the Other World	Altar Permanent fire	Middle
Intermediate Zone *B* Relatively sacred	Tabernacle (south side) Table, candlestick	
Final Limit of This World	Curtain	ground
Other World	Tabernacle (north side) Mercy Seat Ark	Shrine proper

Fig. 9

If you are to understand how the diagram fits the story you will need to pay close attention to what is said in the Exodus references about the construction and lay-out of the Tabernacle and to various cross-references to this design in Leviticus chapters 4, 5 and 6. Although the Tabernacle is represented as a tented structure the authors clearly had in mind a temple building, the groundplan of which would have been not unlike that of many Christian churches but oriented to the north rather than to the east.

86

The precise position of the shrine area in relation to the secular camp is not specified but the implication seems to be that the Tabernacle stands at the centre of the camp which is regarded as the zone of normal Culture, a domesticated tame area contrasted with 'outside the camp', the wilderness zone of wild Nature.

The shrine area as a whole is fenced off from the camp by a rectangular arrangement of hangings (Exodus 27: 9–17). The entrance is on the south side and marked with curtains of bright colours. At the centre of this 'court' is a much more substantial structure with wooden framed walls and tented roof (Exodus 26). The entrance to the tent, similarly marked with bright colours, is again on the south side, and immediately in front of it, in the court, is the altar. This is an elaborate hearth on which a fire, tended by the priest, burns perpetually. The tented structure itself is in two parts divided by a curtain. To the north the Holy of Holies contains the Ark of the Covenant and the Mercy Seat. To the south of the curtain, and thus between the Ark and the altar, is an intermediate sacred area containing the table and the candlestick (Exodus 26: 33–5).

In addition to these various localities inside the camp, there is a vaguely specified 'clean place' somewhere outside the camp, in the wilderness, on which the priest deposits the ashes from the altar fire and other materials which are sufficiently contaminated with sacredness or 'dirt' to be too dangerous to retain within the camp.

The whole of the area within the Tabernacle proper is exclusively reserved for the priests, who must be properly attired and in a ritual state of purity whenever they are tending the altar fire or in the building to the north of it. The restrictions applying to the northern half of the tented area, beyond the curtain, are even more severe.

Great stress is placed upon the details of the priest's dress as a distinguishing mark of his ritual condition. When the priest carries the ash from the altar to the 'clean place outside the camp' he must also wear special clothes, but of a different kind.

Ordinary lay members of the congregation who wish to participate in a ritual may enter the untented 'court of the Tabernacle' but may not pass beyond the altar. All transactions between the lay donor of a sacrificial offering and the altar must be mediated by a priest.

The compatibility of the left half of Fig. 9 with this description is, I hope, clear. In terms of metaphysical topography, the camp represents This World, the Holy of Holies represents the Other World. The Intermediate Zone, which is the focus of active ritual attention, is in two sections, the Court (Zone A) which is relatively secular and free of taboo and the south side of the Tabernacle (Zone B) which is relatively sacred and loaded with taboo. The altar, around which most of the ritual of the Tabernacle is concentrated, stands between these two parts of the Intermediate Zone; it is thus the threshold marking the topographical transition from normal to abnormal, This World to Other.

The fire of the altar is the gateway to the Other World, the channel through which offerings can be transmitted to God, but also the channel through which the power of God can be directly manifested to Man (Leviticus 9: 24; 10: 2).

So much for the setting, but now let us examine the structure of the rituals for which the setting provides a frame. The early chapters of Leviticus are largely concerned with providing prototype rules for the conduct of various types of sacrifice.

Notice how the same elements of ritual behaviour keep on recurring, but linked together in different combinations and different sequences. The elements are like the letters of the alphabet; in different combinations they can be made to say different things.

Leviticus chapter 1 spells out the details of three types of *burnt sacrifice*. The basic difference in the types is in the ranking (i.e. economic cost to the donor) of the victim: (i) a bullock, (ii) a ram or male goat, (iii) a pigeon. In each case the victim's blood is sprinkled around the altar and the door of the Tabernacle and the carcase is cut into portions. The portions are allocated to two categories, (i) an offering, (ii) a residue. The offering consists essentially of the kidneys and the surrounding fat, though in the case of the pigeon it consists of everything except the crop and the feathers. The offering portion is always burnt on the altar; the residue is variously treated. In these particular examples the residue is washed clean of the contents of the stomach and guts (which are put with the ashes of the altar fire) and then burnt.

Chapter 2 describes the procedure for making 'a meat offering to the Lord' which turns out to be a food offering to the priest. The animal is not ritually killed, but a share of meat from a household meal is mixed with ritual oil and flour and frankincense and handed over to the priest; the priest then takes a token portion of the food and burns it on the altar fire. Notice that it is not only the right of the priest to eat this food, it is a duty; for once the food has passed into the hands of the priest it is contaminated with sacredness and too dangerous to take back again into the camp.

Chapter 3 introduces a category called *peace offering*. The procedure for killing the victim is the same as in chapter 1 and the carcase is similarly apportioned, but here only the blood and the offering are handed over to the priest. By implication the donor keeps the rest for himself. However in this chapter certain points about the general procedure are more clearly spelled out. Before the sacrificial animal is killed the donor of the offering invariably establishes a metonymic relationship between himself and the victim by touching the victim on the head. The plain implication is that, in some metaphysical sense, the victim is a vicarious substitution for the donor himself. Notice further that in chapter 3: 17, the composition of the 'offering' portion is used as justification for a general taboo on the eating of fat and blood by members of the Jewish faith.

Chapter 4 discusses *sin offerings* and the role of sacrifice in ritual purification. In this case the distinguishing criterion appears at verse 11. The residue, which was burnt on the altar in chapter 1 and retained by the donor in chapter 3, is here treated as highly contaminated and removed *in toto* to the 'clean place outside the camp' where it is burnt among the ashes from the altar fire.

But now let me go back to the mythological account of the consecration of Aaron and his sons which is given in Leviticus chapters 8–10. Pay close attention not only to who does what to whom but also the order in which the sequence of events is presented. The story presupposes the cosmological–ethnographic context which I have already described. There is a good deal of redundancy and repetition but almost every detail exemplifies one or other of the abstract theoretical principles which have been considered in earlier sections of this essay.

To show this I will lead you through the story verse by verse:

Leviticus (chapter and verse reference)

Chapter 8: 4 The congregation assemble at the door of the Tabernacle (Fig. 9, Intermediate Zone A).

6 The potential initiates (Aaron and his sons) are separated from the congregation and washed with water. Notice that at this stage Moses, who is already established as a priest–mediator who can communicate directly with God, acts as master of ceremonies.

7 Aaron, as principal initiate, is separated from his sons and dressed in special regalia which is specified in detail.

10 The whole of the interior of the Tabernacle, and then the altar and the associated ritual utensils, is sprinkled with ritual oil which is then sprinkled also on Aaron's head (i.e. Aaron is brought into metonymic association with the holy things on the altar). Notice that this anointing and sprinkling with oil is analogous to the sprinkling of the blood of the sacrificial victim (p. 88).

13 The secondary initiates (Aaron's sons) also are dressed in special clothes.

14 The bullock of the sin offering is then produced and Aaron and his sons touch the head of the bullock with their hands.

15–17 Moses sacrifices the bullock in accordance with the rules laid down in chapter 4.

89

18–21 Moses sacrifices "the ram for the burnt offering" in accordance with the rules laid down in chapter 1 (p. 88). The bullock (sin offering) of verse 14 and the ram (burnt offering) of verse 18 need to be seen as a linked pair, analogous to the pair of pigeons in Leviticus chapter 5: 7–10. The two sacrifices are similar but different; the overall implication is the already redundant theme of 'separation', especially separation of purity from impurity.

You may here find it useful to look back at Fig. 7 (p. 78). We have now completed the initial 'rite of separation'.

22 A further ram is now produced which is described as 'the ram of consecration'. Here the identification of the ram with Aaron and his sons is pursued even more systematically than before (verse 24) but when the 'offering' portion of the victim's carcase has been separated it is not burnt in the usual way by the priest, but is first handed over to Aaron and his sons. After the initiates have waved the dish containing the offering over the altar, Moses, as priest, takes it back again and its contents are then burnt as before.

29 Moses himself goes through a similar 'waving' performance with the 'breast' of the ram – i.e. with a part of the carcase that would otherwise be treated as 'residue' – but does *not* burn it.

30 A further annointing with oil and blood repeats the same message – Aaron is identified with the *offering* portion of the victim's carcase, *not* with the *residue*.

31 Moses now hands over the meat of the 'residue' to Aaron and his sons and instructs them to cook and eat this within the confines of the Tabernacle and to stay in confinement there for seven days. Here look again at Fig. 7 (p. 78). We have now reached the end of the *rite de marge* and the newly consecrated priest must be brought back into society in his new social status by a rite of aggregation.

Chapter 9: 1–4 There is a further series of sacrifices paired as before (see comment on chapter 8: 18–21 above):

(i)   a sin offering (young calf) ⎱
(ii) a burnt offering (ram) ⎰ with Aaron as donor

(iii) a sin offering (kid goat)   ⎱ with the whole congregation as
(iv) a burnt offering (calf and lamb) ⎰ donor

(v)   a meat offering (verse 17) ⎱
(vi) a peace offering ⎰ for the whole congregation

The proceedings are the same as those described in chapter 8 with the difference that Aaron now performs all the priestly functions which had previously been assigned to Moses.

The culmination comes at verse 24 where the effectiveness of Aaron's priestly ministrations is shown by the fact that 'a fire came out from before the Lord and consumed the burnt offering and fat upon the altar'. This manifestation of divine power is appropriately accompanied by noise – 'the people shouted' (cf. p. 63).

But remember that, according to the mythical – metaphysical representation of the proceedings, Aaron himself is the victim who has been transmitted to the Other World to establish a channel of communication with the deity, so in order to get back again to normality in his new priestly status, Aaron must sacrifice (shed by separation) a part of himself.

Chapter 10: 1–5 So the myth has the two sons Nadab and Abihu destroyed by the fire of the Lord. Their bodies are not treated as normal human corpses but as the residue of a sin offering i.e. they are taken outside the camp without ceremony. That this myth expresses the idea of purification through sacrifice rather than divine retribution is made clear by the fact that the imperfect sons Nadab and Abihu are promptly replaced by perfected sons Eleazar and Ithamar (verse 12). Moreover the account of the destruction of Nadab and Abihu (verses 1–7) is immediately followed by a homily on the importance of putting a 'difference between holy and unholy and between clean and unclean'.

Incidentally this structuralist view which makes Eleazar and Ithamar a 'replacement' of Nadab and Abihu rather than separate characters provides an explanation for the otherwise puzzling argument of chapter 10: 16–20. The 'sin offering in the holy place' which Eleazar and Ithamar fail to eat is, by substitution, the bodies of their dead brothers, or by further substitution, themselves!

I want you now to skip a few chapters and take a close look at Leviticus chapter 16, which describes the procedure for the sacrifice of the scapegoat. The point that I want you to appreciate is that this seemingly anomalous form of sacrifice is simply a transformation of what has been described before which fits in with the same set of cosmological ideas and the same set of metaphoric and metonymic associations.

The basic theme is that, since God himself is liable to be present on the Mercy Seat in the Holy of Holies, even Aaron as high priest can only enter the northern end of the Tabernacle (Fig. 9, p. 86) after specially elaborate rituals of purification.

Five sacrificial animals are involved altogether:

(i)   a sin offering (bullock) ⎱
(ii) a burnt offering (ram)   ⎰ with Aaron as donor (verse 3)

(iii) a sin offering (two goats) ⎱ with the whole congregation as donor
(iv) a burnt offering (a ram)   ⎰ (verse 5)

The special feature in this case is that the two goats in (iii) are first distinguished by chance – that is by divine intervention (verses 8–10)

– and then differently treated. The general procedure with the animals *other than* the goat which has been selected as scapegoat (verse 8) is the same as before, except that the blood sprinkling is specifically stated to extend into the Holy of Holies and to include the Mercy Seat, but the scapegoat is the object of a special ritual (verses 21–2). By means of a magical verbal spell the sins of the congregation are collectively transferred to the goat. The goat is then taken away into the uninhabited wilderness and abandoned alive.

The other goat and the bullock are treated as ordinary sin offerings as in chapter 4 (see above, p. 89).

Taken as a whole the scapegoat sequence is the exact converse of the Aaron sequence. Aaron, separated step by step from the secular contaminations of the congregation and his own imperfections, ends up pure and holy at the centre of the camp. The scapegoat, having been separated step by step from other goats and other sacrificial animals, is loaded with the contaminations from which the congregation and Aaron have been freed and then ends up impure and unholy (but nevertheless 'sacred') far out in the wilderness.

The central principle is that the separation of spiritual essence from material body at death is paradigmatic of the mechanism which 'causes' a change of social status among the living. The repeated use of animal sacrifices to mark stages of transition in all kinds of rites of passage exploits this paradigm.

But conversely, in the scapegoat case, we need a symbol for a creature which is removed from the ritual stage but is *not* separated from its impurities. It is therefore appropriate that the scapegoat should *not* be killed.

I hope I have persuaded you that, in the analysis of ethnography, attention to small details really matters.

Some of you may wonder how far, if at all, these very general interpretative statements can be applied to Christian rituals.

Sacrifice in Christianity appears only in vicarious symbolic form as a reference to mythology. According to the myth, the god–man Christ was murdered by men of evil intent. But by a complex transformation this has retrospectively become a sacrifice, in that the murder was willed by God. The sacrifice is now a persisting channel through which the grace of God can flow to the devout believer. The donor of the sacrifice is Christ himself and the priest, in offering the bread and wine to the congregation as 'the body and blood of Christ', is, by implication, timelessly repeating the sacrifice at the behest of the divine Donor.

Because we happen to know a great deal about the history of Christianity we can see that the cross-references and symbolic transformations in this particular case have been exceedingly involved. The Christian Mass, as a whole, is a transformation of the Jewish Passover, and the crucified Christ 'is' the sacrificial paschal lamb, 'the Lamb of God'. The bread and wine is on this account associated with the meat of the sacrifice not only by metaphor but also by metonymy (cf. Leviticus 23).

These issues are extremely complex but even so I would point out that the metaphor, which I have analysed, whereby Aaron himself has to suffer the pangs of sacrifice before he can become fully effective as a permanent intermediary between God on His Mercy Seat and the sinful suffering congregation, is structurally very close indeed to the Christian idea that Jesus must die before he becomes fully effective as a permanent mediator between God and suffering mankind.

The theological literature on the subject is vast but anthropologically naïve. Anthropological analysis of a modern kind is sparse. A paper which adopts, in some respects, the terminology of this present essay is Fernandez (1974).

19. *Conclusion*

Now that we have come to the end I suggest that you go back to the beginning and re-read my Introduction and then decide how far I have fulfilled my promises.

The purpose of the long discussion of sacrifice in Section 18 was to illustrate my original assertions that 'detail is the essence of the matter', 'every detail of custom must be seen as part of a complex', 'details, considered in isolation, are as meaningless as isolated letters of the alphabet'. But let us consider this analogy with letters of the alphabet more closely. What is the process by which we make letters convey information? We first select twenty-six marks from an infinity of possible marks and declare that these twenty-six marks constitute a set. Then we make an inventory of the sounds of our spoken language, cutting up the intonation continuum in a distinctly arbitrary way. We then allocate the arbitrarily distinguished sounds to the arbitrarily distinguished letter marks, and tidy things up by improvising a number of special combinations for sounds which will not fit. Then finally, by stringing the letters together in sequences, we produce a kind of model of natural speech or at any rate of an idealised version of natural speech.

If you think carefully about the evidence provided by my sacrifice example you will see that the analogy goes quite a long way. The elements of the ritual ('the letters of the alphabet') do not mean anything in themselves; they come to have meaning by virtue of contrast with other elements. Furthermore, just as the contrasted letters can only be combined into meaningful patterns if they are confined to a specific setting – e.g. a linear arrangement on a sheet of paper – so also the contrasted elements of ritual can be recombined in diverse ways to produce total messages, but only if the recombination takes place within a common overall setting, the structure of which is presupposed by the way the combinations are made, both spatially and sequentially.

But having made this point I would urge you to treat the analogy between ritual and language, or at any rate between ritual and written language, with some caution.

The heart of my argument is that non-verbal communication is ordinarily achieved in the way that the conductor of an orchestra conveys musical information to his listeners, and *not* in the way that the writer of a book conveys verbal information to his readers (cf. Section 9). A derivative major proposition is that signs and symbols convey meaning in combination and not just as sets of binary signs in linear sequence or sets of metaphoric symbols in paradigmatic association. Or, to put the same point differently, we must know a lot about the cultural context, the setting of the stage, before we can even begin to decode the message.

In this respect my argument is I think compatible with the general position of Mary Douglas and with the vastly more detailed analyses of Victor Turner. But it needs to be clearly distinguished from the position of Firth (1973). Firth devotes separate chapters of his book to 'Food Symbolism', 'Hair Symbolism', 'Bodily Symbols of Greeting and Parting', 'Symbolism of Flags', Symbolism of Gift Exchange'. Each category of symbols is discussed by itself, and within each category each symbolic usage is itemised by particular example. The nearest that I come to such a procedure in this essay is in Section 13 where clothing, colour, cooking and bodily mutilations are discussed as alternative expressions of 'the same' binary oppositions; i.e. my thesis is that each of these codes is potentially a transformation of any of the others.

The general set of ideas involved in the concept of *structural transformation* seems to me quite fundamental. The particular terminological jargon which I have adopted in Section 2 is designed to make the concept of transformation reasonably comprehensive. Those who prefer to use a different set of category distinctions should bear this in mind.

On the negative side the reader will notice that my essay contains no reference at all to Freud. Psycho-analytic theory claims to provide a causal explanation of how private (nonce) symbols are connected, but since it is argued, reasonably enough, that all culturally standardised symbols must have started out as nonce symbols, psycho-analysts often claim to be able to 'explain' culturally standardised symbols as well.

In several earlier publications, notably Leach (1958, 1972), I have considered how far psycho-analytic and structuralist–anthropological interpretations of symbolic connections are mutually compatible. My general conclusion is that the hunches of psycho-analysts are probably quite often correct, but that the 'theory' by which they seek to justify their hunches is of such intellectual crudity and so lacking in sophistication that it has practically no value as a general tool for the analysis of ethnographic materials. On the other hand many Freudian-type

96

interpretations of symbolic behaviour are perfectly compatible with the theory outlined in this present essay.

This is an issue about which serious social anthropologists need to think very carefully but it is not a matter which can be handled satisfactorily within the space available to me here.

My final positive suggestion to my undergraduate readers is that, armed with the analytical apparatus which this essay provides, you should now go back to one of the great classical monographs of social anthropology and consider whether it gets you any further. For example, does Leach (1971) add anything to Radcliffe-Brown (1922)? I think it does.

Bibliography

(a) The following items have been mentioned either explicitly or by implication in the body of the text.

Barth, Fredrik (1966), *Models of Social Organization* (Royal Anthropological Institute: Occasional Paper no. 23). London: Royal Anthropological Institute.

Barthes, Roland (1967), *Elements of Semiology*, trans. A. Lavers and C. Smith. London: Cape Editions.

Bauman, R. (1974), 'Speaking in the Light: the Role of the Quaker Minister' in R. Bauman and J. Sherzer (eds.), *Explorations in the Ethnography of Speaking*. Cambridge: Cambridge University Press.

Cassirer, Ernst (1953–7), *Philosophy of Symbolic Forms*, 3 vols., trans. R. Manheim. New Haven: Yale University Press.

Douglas, Mary (1966), *Purity and Danger*. London: Routledge and Kegan Paul.

(1970), *Natural Symbols*. London: Cresset Press.

(1972), 'Symbolic orders in the use of domestic space' in Peter J. Ucko, Ruth Tringham and G. W. Dimbleby, *Man, Settlement and Urbanism*, pp. 513–21. Cambridge (Mass.): Schenkman Publishing Co.

Evans-Pritchard, E. E. (1956), *Nuer Religion*. Oxford: Clarendon Press.

Fernandez, J. W. (1965), 'Symbolic consensus in a Fang reformative cult', *American Anthropologist*, 67: 902–29.

(1974), 'The mission of metaphor in expressive culture', *Current Anthropology*, 15: 119–45.

Firth, Raymond (1973), *Symbols; Public and Private*. London: Allen and Unwin.

Geertz, C. (1973), 'Thick Description: Toward an Interpretive Theory of Culture' in Clifford Geertz, *The Interpretation of Cultures: Selected Essays by Clifford Geertz*, pp. 3–30. New York: Basic Books Inc.

Hjelmslev, L. (1953), *Prolegomena to a Theory of Language*. Bloomington: Indiana University Press.

99

Jakobson, R. and Halle, M. (1956), *Fundamentals of Language* (Janua Linguarum: Series Minor 1). The Hague: Mouton.

Leach, E. R. (1954), *Political Systems of Highland Burma*. London: G. Bell and Sons Ltd.

(1958), 'Magical hair', *Journal of the Royal Anthropological Institute*, 88: 147–64.

(1961), *Pul Eliya: A Village in Ceylon*. Cambridge: Cambridge University Press.

(1964), 'Anthropological aspects of language: animal categories and verbal abuse', in E. H. Lenneberg (ed.), *New Directions in the Study of Language*. Cambridge (Mass.): MIT Press.

(1970), *Claude Lévi-Strauss*. New York: Viking Press; London: Fontana.

(1971), '*Kimil:* A Category of Andamanese Thought', in P. Maranda and E. K. Maranda (eds.), *Structural Analysis of Oral Tradition*. Philadelphia: University of Pennsylvania Press.

(1972), 'The Structure of Symbolism' in J. S. La Fontaine (ed.), *The Interpretation of Ritual*. London: Tavistock Publications.

Lévi-Strauss, C. (1949), *Les Structures élémentaires de la parenté*. Paris: P.U.F.

(1955), 'The Structural Study of Myth', *Journal of American Folklore*, 68, no. 270. (A revised version appears as chapter 11 of Lévi-Strauss, 1963.)

(1962), *Totemism*, trans. R. Needham. London: Merlin Press.

(1963), *Structural Anthropology*, trans. C. Jacobson and B. G. Schoepf. New York: Basic Books Inc.

(1966 (a)), *The Savage Mind*. Chicago: University of Chicago Press.

(1966(b)), 'The Culinary Triangle', *New Society* (London), 22 December, 166: 937–40.

(1966(c)), *Mythologiques 2: Du Miel aux Cendres*. Paris: Plon.

(1970), *The Raw and the Cooked*, trans. J. and D. Weightman. London: Jonathan Cape.

Malinowski, B. (1922), *Argonauts of the Western Pacific*. London: Routledge and Kegan Paul.

Maranda, E. K. and Maranda, P. (1971), *Structural Models in Folklore and Transformational Essays*. The Hague: Mouton.

Mauss, Marcel (1954), *The Gift*, trans. Ian Cunnison. London: Cohen and West.

Mauss, M. and Beuchat, M. H. (1906), 'Essai sur les variations saisonnières des sociétés Eskimos', *L'Année sociologique 1904–5*, 9.

Morris, Charles (1971), *Writings of the General Theory of Signs* (Approaches to Semiotics 16). The Hague: Mouton.

Mulder, J. W. F. and Hervey, S. G. J. (1972), *Theory of the Linguistic*

Sign (Janua Linguarum: Series Minor 136). The Hague: Mouton.

Needham, R. (ed.) (1973), *Right and Left: Essays in Dual Symbolic Classification*. Chicago: University of Chicago Press.

O'Flaherty, W. D. (1973), *Asceticism and Eroticism in the Mythology of Siva*. London: Oxford University Press.

Peirce, C. S. (1931–5), *Collected Papers of Charles Sanders Peirce*, ed. C. Harteshorne and P. Weiss. Cambridge (Mass.): Harvard University Press.

Radcliffe-Brown, A. R. (1922), *The Andaman Islanders*. Cambridge: Cambridge University Press.

Saussure, F. de (1966), *Course in General Linguistics*, Ed. C. Bally, A. Sechehaye, A. Riedlinger, trans. Wade Baskin. New York: McGraw-Hill Paperbacks.

Turner, V. W. (1967), *The Forest of Symbols*. Ithaca: Cornell University Press.

Wolf, A. P. (1970), 'Chinese Kinship and Mourning Dress' in M. Freedman (ed.), *Family and Kinship in Chinese Society*, pp. 189–208. Stanford: Stanford University Press.

(b) Suggestions for further reading.

Even a cursory examination of the long bibliographies provided by Firth (1973) and Fernandez (1974) will indicate the enormous range of reading matter which is potentially relevant to the theme of this essay. Further reading must therefore largely depend upon the special interests of the reader. The items listed below are mostly symposia of collected essays. Apart from the items dealing explicitly with the mathematical theory of communication they have been chosen because they give emphasis to visual, psychological and ethnological aspects of human communication which are under-represented in reference list (a).

Birdwhistell, R. (1970), *Kinesics and Context*. Philadelphia: University of Pennsylvania Press.

Gumperz, J. J. and Hymes, D. (eds.) (1964), *The Ethnography of Communication: American Anthropologist Special Publication*, vol. 66, no. 6, part 2.

(1972), *Directions in Sociolinguistics: The Ethnography of Communication*. New York: Holt, Rinehart and Winston Inc.

Hinde, R. A. (ed.) (1972), *Non-Verbal Communication*. Cambridge: Cambridge University Press.

Jung, C. G. (ed.) (1964), *Man and his Symbols*. London: Aldus Books Ltd and W. H. Allen and Co.

Kepes, G. (ed.) (1966), *Sign, Image and Symbol*. London: Studio Vista.

Marshak, A. (1972), *The Roots of Civilisation: The Cognitive Beginnings of Man's First Art, Symbol and Notation.* London: Weidenfeld and Nicholson.

Minnis, N. (ed.) (1971), *Linguistics at Large.* New York: The Viking Press.

Pierce, J. R. (1962), *Symbols, Signals and Noise.* London: Hutchinson.

Romney, A. K. and D'Andrade, R. G. (eds.) (1964), *Transcultural Studies in Cognition: American Anthropologist: Special Publication,* vol. 66, no. 3, part 2.

Smith, A. G. (ed.) (1966), *Communication and Culture: readings in the codes of human interaction.* New York: Holt, Rinehart and Winston.

Willis, R. (ed.) (1975); *The Interpretation of Symbolism* (ASA Studies). London: Malaby Press.

Index